THE WAY OF
THE WARRIOR

9

THE WAY OF THE WARRIOR

The Dark Secrets of
the Samurai Code

Jōtarō

CITADEL PRESS
Kensington Publishing Corp.
www.kensingtonbooks.com

CITADEL PRESS BOOKS are published by

Kensington Publishing Corp.
119 West 40th Street
New York, NY 10018

All Kensington titles, imprints, and distributed lines are available at special quantity discounts for bulk purchases for sales promotions, premiums, fund-raising, educational, or institutional use. Special book excerpts or customized printings can also be created to fit specific needs. For details, write or phone the office of the Kensington special sales manager: Kensington Publishing Corp., 119 West 40th Street, New York, NY 10018, attn: Special Sales Department; phone 1-800-221-2647.

First printing: May 2011

10 9 8 7 6 5 4 3 2 1

Printed in the United States of Am

CIP data is available.

ISBN-13: 978-0-8065-3232-5
ISBN-10: 0-8065-3232-7

For A~

Contents

PART FIVE: VOID

THE WAY OF THE WARRIOR

PART ONE

Foundation

1. IN THE BEGINNING . . .

"**I was with you** in the beginning," said the master, "long before we first met." The student did not understand this at first,
but in the time they had spent together, he came to appreciate that any truth worth knowing would likely take some time
to grasp. He responded as he had been taught to—with the
known. "We were together at the training camp." It was really
a statement, not a question, but both men were familiar with
this particular didactic paradigm. The master nodded his
agreement. "And before that at the university"—again, a curt
nod—"but before that . . ." the question trailed away into
nothingness.

"Think," the master commanded with an uncharacteristic
hint of urgency. "Our paths have crossed many times over the

years." The student was at a loss. In another time and place, he would have been sent away to ponder this impenetrable proposition, perhaps revisiting the issue on several occasions before arriving at an answer, but now time was growing short for the pair. "Before that I was alone," he said, with a touch more sadness in his voice than he intended. "Were you?" came the inevitable reply.

The student cast his mind back over the years to a time when the master was unknown to him. A time when he inhabited a world where he believed everything his eyes and ears told him and trusted in nothing beyond that limited perspective. It was hard in many ways to remember, like a sighted man trying to recall his blindness. Had there been nothing more than waking, working, eating, and sleeping? He sat still and silent in a way that was physically impossible and psychologically uncomfortable for the vast majority of the population, and closed his eyes. It took only a few moments to overcome the body's natural tendency to peer into the resulting blackness with the eyes and to allow his mind to reach out its tendrils and begin to probe the murky depths.

Time passed. It might have been seconds or hours. At last an image began to form. He was a child on a train traveling through the night toward some distant destination. After his mother had fallen asleep, he stole his way back down the swaying corridors to the caboose, where the conductors sat huddled around a stove playing cards. At first, they had ignored him, but as the night wore on, the oldest of them showed him a trick. Allowing the wide-eyed boy to choose any card he had liked from the fanned-out deck, the old man named his selection time after time, without the slightest hint of artifice. Try as he might, the young one could not figure it out. When pressed, the conjurer finally explained that there was no trick—just his natural ability to force the observer to select the card he wanted. This had been the student's first encounter with the art. But had the master been there? Had he even known of the incident? The student could not recall ever mentioning it and had even forgotten it himself until just now.

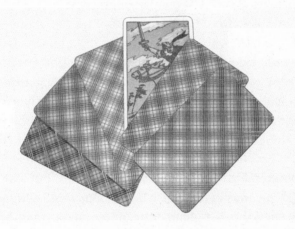

Another image swam into his mind of him walking to the junior school as a young boy, passing the same homeless fellow day after day, month after month, year after year, just sitting on a park bench, rocking back and forth, and listening to a radio that never made a sound. He even dropped some loose change at the man's feet on occasion. Then came the day when a lady screamed and a young man ran past, her stolen purse swinging wildly from his tightly clenched fists. With surprising speed the homeless man had flipped a gold shield on a chain around the collar of his tattered flannel shirt, barked a few crisp orders into his handheld radio, and given chase. This was the student's first glimpse into the shadow world. He had no recollection of the master's presence there, but he had long ago come to realize that things were rarely what they seemed.

A third scene played itself out against the backdrop of his closed lids. He saw a tortured skeleton of a boy at the military academy, the one with no friends, no family, no talent, and no hope. The total indifference of the officers and instructors to the outcast's agony. His own attempts to befriend this boy, who no one else would, were useless. And his efforts were viewed by others with scorn. His was the ultimate failure. And the eerie creaking from the rafters of the darkened gymnasium where they had finally found him. This had been the student's first, faltering step along the way. He could recall no sign of the master in that harsh and unforgiving environment. And yet the impulse to protect must have come from somewhere.

He ventured a guess. "Your art? Your world? Your way?"

"Close," the master replied. "Our art. Our world. Our way." And with that, the first glimmering of true understanding began to take hold.

2. *JUTSU* AND *DO* — THE SHADOW WARRIOR

He who fights with monsters might take care lest he
thereby become a monster. And if you gaze for long
into an abyss, the abyss gazes also into you.

—Friedrich Nietzsche

The student—or more accurately the graduate—was in a
dark place. Since his last encounter with the master, his path
had taken him deep into the shadow world and pitted him
against powerful and dangerous adversaries, in a war that
raged beyond the range of most people's limited perception.
At first it had seemed challenging and exciting, but of late it
began to wear on him and to eat at his soul. As the philoso-
pher cautions, when you look into the abyss, you must take
care, for in so doing, the abyss looks also into you. He might
not have come to seek the master's counsel of his own

6

accord, but, as is often the case, fate made the decision for him, summoning him to his former teacher's bedside.

He had scarcely entered the room before the master observed, "You are troubled." In the space of those first few seconds, the graduate's years of experience seemed to melt away, and he felt again like a child in the presence of a parent. Dispensing with the usual pleasantries, he explained the cause of his inner turmoil as best he could. In essence it came down to this: How was it possible to combat the forces of darkness, day in, day out, without in some way resorting to their tactics or at some level succumbing to their deadly allure? Ultimately, what distinguished the deep-cover operative from the criminal; the freedom fighter from the terrorist; or the soldier from the assassin?

The master pondered this question for a time. Then he reached for the green bottle of medicine by his bed and poured a large measure of the viscous liquid into his half-filled teacup. The student averted his eyes respectfully from this necessary interruption. But the master's command refocused his attention. "Shake," he said. The student did as he was told. When the task was complete, the student lifted his palm from the top of the cup and looked inside. The murky mixture had taken on the properties of both liquids: the pale amber of the tea blending with the sage pigmentation of the medicine, to produce a homogenous, swirling, mucky, brown soup. He glanced back toward the master. "Look closer," he said. The student held the glass up to the light and peered at it again. From this improved vantage point, he could make out tiny, oily beads of the elixir scattered in suspension throughout the volume of the thin, transparent beverage.

"There is light and there is darkness," the master began, "*yin* and *yang*, *in* and *yo*. But these ideas are not as simple as 'good' and 'evil' as you understand them. There are times when great danger thrives in daylight and when salvation comes from the shadows. These principles are relative, and they depend on each other for their very existence, for in yin, there is yang, and in yang, there is yin. Balancing these two elements, that is your task. But no matter how closely they blend, each retains its fundamental"—he struggled for a moment searching for the right word—"character."

"Long before I gave you the weapons of the shadow warrior, I armed you with the wisdom to use them honorably. That is why you learned to walk the way before you came to know the art within. Think back to our first lessons." The student noted that he did not say, "Our first meeting." He cast back his mind down the corridor of changing seasons to those long, lazy, idyllic summer days at the university and the life-changing discovery he had made at the end of the rickety railway line on the densely wooded outskirts of the nearby village.

3. *KISHIDO*—THE WAY OF THE WESTERN WARRIOR

There are many paths to the top of the mountain, but the view is always the same.

—Chinese proverb

When the master first coined the term *Kishido*, characteristically he chose not to explain it.[1] Only a sense of its meaning could be gathered from the context in which he employed it. Some time later, he painted the character with brush and ink,

1. For the reader's convenience, words and expressions drawn from other languages (except those appearing in a standard English dictionary) will generally be italicized the first time they appear in the text, and their definitions may be found in the glossary.

for a *hachimaki* design. The terminal symbol for the Way, *-do*, was familiar, but the prefix was a mystery. It contained the cross-shaped symbol meaning gentleman and the peculiar letter *E* character with a tail and four little strokes denoting a reference to matters equestrian. But the collective meaning in the elegant arrangement of radicals was only revealed by reference to a well-worn *kanji* dictionary: *kishi*, "an English knight." At first, this linguistic acknowledgment of the British students in his decidedly Japanese *dojo* was merely pleasing and amusing, but with the passage of time, the profundity of his pronouncement became clear.

The master knew that as university students his "Englishmen" were only likely to enjoy the benefit of his teaching for a season before graduating and setting out on the journeys of their young lives. He recognized that there was scarcely time to impart a modicum of proficiency in the arts he taught, let alone to strip away decades of contrasting experiences born of an entirely alien society, so as to begin again with tabula rasa. His adoption of the term Kishido, therefore, reflected a broad-minded willingness to accept his students' existing cultural, and, for some, martial traditions, and to add his unique script to that slate. To blend the ingredients.

Some say that if you wish to learn the deep truth of a martial way, you must live in the nation of its origin. They say that to penetrate the soul of an art you must study it exhaustively and exclusively. This is a sound position. Their dedication is to be admired, and their wisdom sought out. They are the professors of their particular disciplines. But theirs is not the only way. Some people are nomads by choice or circumstance. Their quest takes them all across the globe, rarely staying in one place long enough to grow roots. The gypsy lifestyle provides quite an eclectic education, but it also presents difficulties for the novice who wishes to embark upon such a demanding odyssey as the study of any true martial art. As a result, the student's progress is slow and onerous, but for the dedicated, it is also inexorable.

While an itinerant apprentice must strive to realize depth in his studies, achieving breadth is almost unavoidable. Acclimatizing to each new location requires the conscious acquisition and digestion of a multitude of data and skills—matters that more established residents may take for granted. Admission to each new art or style requires adherents to divest themselves of preconceived notions and to see again through new eyes. This arrangement fosters a broad view, which, in turn, provides valuable insight into the *gestält* of the matter.

In tracing the origin of the Eastern martial tradition, the historian will generally arrive at Damo's apocryphal journey from India to China in the sixth century AD, and with it the advent of the fundamental elements of Zen Buddhism and the seeds of the legendary exercises of the monks at Shaolin. What is less well known, however, is that Greek warriors, trained in the art of Pankrateon (either ground wrestling or standing fighting), had previously influenced Indian martial practices when the armies of Alexander the Great invaded that country in 326 BC. The historical interplay between the Western and Eastern traditions endures in such systems as Filipino Arnis de Mano, a term derived from the European word "harness"[2] and an art, which legend has it, that Chief Lapulapu employed to dispatch Magellan on Mactan Island in 1521, during the Spanish invasion. Such salutary symbiosis is also manifest in the refined blend of Chinese and Western boxing common to many modern styles and perhaps best exemplified by the art of Wei Kuen Do. So the great wheel turns and turns again.

If that had been the master's only point, he might have chosen to adopt an expression meaning the universal way. But he did not. He chose a term that referred specifically to the European tradition. In time, it became clear that he had a peculiar affinity for British culture, particularly the reserved, deferential, and altogether gentle ethos that yet held sway within the walls of the ancient university, if nowhere else in the last vestiges of empire. It was, after all, among the reasons he found himself so far away from his home, teaching and living in that most unusual place.

The Japanese finishing school at which he taught, complete with traditional architecture and authentic *shaho*, was somewhat out of place as well as time, hidden away in the

2. Referring to a device for girding the sword.

English countryside, but then again, the nearby university was also something of an anachronism. Although the idea of the finishing school was, at least in principle, to expose Japanese youth to British culture, Westerners rarely passed through the stone outer markers that stood like stern sentinels at the end of the winding, wooded entrance. The master decided after a time that a few of his British students should be permitted to enter. The collision of cultures was marked, but it also reflected a certain symmetry. There was a common ground. Those who met in that revered location were of a mind.

If this had been the extent of the master's insight, he might have chosen an expression simply meaning the Western way. But he did not. He chose a term that embraced the whole of the ancient European martial tradition: the knight's way; the Way of the Western Warrior. Upon reflection, the reason for this semantic distinction became apparent. Parallels emerged: the elegant taper and graceful devastation of both the *yumi* and the yew longbow; the *samurai* art of *bajutsu*; the chevalier's study of dressage; the wearing of *daisho* in feudal Japan; the use of the rapier and *main gauche* (a dagger) in Renaissance Europe; the *koshi mawari* common to both *oi tsuki* and a good straight right; and, perhaps most important of all, the themes common to both *bushido* and the chivalric code.

With a masterstroke, Kishido mixed two vibrant, primary colors, to produce a third altogether new shade, while retaining the beauty of its constituent antecedents. Supplement Sun Tzu with Carl von Clausewitz. Study Miyamoto Musashi's *Go Rin No Sho* alongside Giacomo di Grasse's *His True Arte of Defence* and Vincentio Saviolo's *his Practise*. Contrast Morikawa's *Hanare* and Junsei Yoshimi's *Shahokun* with George Agar

Hansard's *Book of Archery*. None is inherently superior. Each is a valuable travelogue of the author's particular path. And each path represents a different route to the same mountain-top.

Kishido has contained in its suffix and linguistic structure the extensive and venerable Oriental martial tradition; yet within its sense and substance dwells the heart of the European heroic ideal. For the Western warrior, it feels a lot like home.

4. *BUMON*—LINEAGE

I like a man who grins when he fights.

—Sir Winston Churchill

With its roots in Arthurian legend and its culmination in the valiant and sometimes single-handed British defense of Europe during World War II, the history and traditions of the European theater of warfare provide a rich resource for the student of the martial arts. It is perhaps with the apocryphal Oath of *Logres*—the philosophical component of the temporal Kingdom of Camelot in sixth-century Britain—that the concept of a knight's way first emerges. Like bushido, however, the composition and emphasis of the warrior's code, as well as his art, has evolved significantly over time.

Baptized by fire while still a child and then grown into a master strategist, Charlemagne ruled the larger part of ninth-century Europe at the height of his power. Following in the footsteps of Hannibal, Charles the Great dared to cross the Alps in AD 773 to expedite the invasion of Lombardy, and his campaigns over the following two decades yielded victory upon victory across the breadth of the continent. Some military historians ascribe these astounding conquests to a series of rapid marches across treacherous terrain, thereby capturing the element of surprise or, at least, advantageous timing. Others, however, suggest that Charlemagne owed his success as much to moral ascendancy as he did to mere physical or mental superiority, deriving this higher mandate, at least in part, from his inspirational communications with Pope Adrian I.

The image of Charlemagne as a military genius, according to the historian Thomas Bullfinch, is incomplete without corresponding attention to his ensuing "mood of peace." At the conclusion of his campaigns, Charlemagne turned his attention to agriculture, legislation, education, and the affairs of state. He founded a royal academy for directing the studies of all schools of the kingdom, and what is more, in the tradition of the Round Table, Charlemagne made himself a member of this body with equal standing to all others. No surprise, therefore, that both aspects of the great leader are reflected in his Chivalric Code, one of the earliest written records describing the essence of knightly duty:

The Chivalric Code of Charlemagne
To serve God and defend the Church
To serve the liege lord in valour and faith
To protect the weak and defenceless
To give succour to widows and orphans
To refrain from the wanton giving of offence
To live by honour and for glory
To despise pecuniary reward

To fight for the welfare of all
To obey those justly in authority
To guard the honour of fellow knights
To eschew unfairness, meanness, and deceit
To keep faith
At all times to speak the truth
To persevere to the end any enterprise begun
To respect the honour of women
Never to refuse a challenge from an equal
Never to turn the back upon a foe

The Bow

The advent of the British longbow radically upset the balance of power on the field of medieval warfare during the Hundred Years' War (1337–1453). Mastery of this weapon, however, required significant dedication, both mental as well as physical. The rigors demanded of the longbow men are evidenced by the physical deformations discovered in the remains of an archer aboard the *Mary Rose*, a Tudor warship sunk in Portsmouth Harbor in 1545. The bones of his left forearm showed compression thickening, the upper spine was twisted radially, and the tips of the first few fingers of his right hand were markedly thickened. These were the same digits that the captors of many archers would amputate; a practice which some say led to the use of the vulgar V gesture by British soldiers to express scorn or derision for their enemy, in effect flaunting the very instrumentalities of his imminent undoing.

At Crécy in 1346, at Poitiers in 1356, and, again, at Agincourt in 1415, English longbow men soundly defeated larger and more heavily armed opposing forces. Notwithstanding the historical significance of these victories, of perhaps even greater import to the canon of the European martial tradition are the principles articulated in Shakespeare's fictionalized retelling of one such tale. As the bard would have it, on the eve of battle, King Henry V has disguised himself and wanders among his soldiers to discern their mood. The Earl of Westmoreland laments the odds facing the beleaguered British force. The king replies. What follows is perhaps the most eloquent expression of the principles of courage, honor, generosity, tradition, and brotherhood in the English language:

King Henry V

What's he that wishes so?
My cousin Westmoreland? No, my fair cousin:
If we are mark'd to die, we are enow
To do our country loss; and if to live,
The fewer men, the greater share of honour.
God's will! I pray thee, wish not one man more.
By Jove, I am not covetous for gold,
Nor care I who doth feed upon my cost;
It yearns me not if men my garments wear;
Such outward things dwell not in my desires:
But if it be a sin to covet honour,
I am the most offending soul alive.
No, faith, my coz, wish not a man from England:
God's peace! I would not lose so great an honour
As one man more, methinks, would share from me
For the best hope I have. O, do not wish one more!
Rather proclaim it, Westmoreland, through my host,
That he which hath no stomach to this fight,
Let him depart; his passport shall be made
And crowns for convoy put into his purse:
We would not die in that man's company
That fears his fellowship to die with us.
This day is called the feast of Crispian:

He that outlives this day, and comes safe home,
Will stand a tip-toe when the day is named,
And rouse him at the name of Crispian.
He that shall live this day, and see old age,
Will yearly on the vigil feast his neighbours,
And say "To-morrow is Saint Crispian:"
Then will he strip his sleeve and show his scars.
And say "These wounds I had on Crispin's day."
Old men forget: yet all shall be forgot,
But he'll remember with advantages
What feats he did that day: then shall our names.
Familiar in his mouth as household words
Harry the king, Bedford and Exeter,
Warwick and Talbot, Salisbury and Gloucester,
Be in their flowing cups freshly remember'd.
This story shall the good man teach his son;
And Crispin Crispian shall ne'er go by,
From this day to the ending of the world,
But we in it shall be remember'd;
We few, we happy few, we band of brothers;
For he to-day that sheds his blood with me
Shall be my brother; be he ne'er so vile,
This day shall gentle his condition:
And gentlemen in England now a-bed
Shall think themselves accursed they were not here,
And hold their manhoods cheap whiles any speaks
That fought with us upon Saint Crispin's day.

—Act IV, Scene III

The Horse

Military historians generally agree that the age of the ascendancy of cavalry in Europe began with the battle of

Adrianople in AD 378, when Gothic horsemen annihilated the legions of the Roman emperor Valens. One of the earliest treatises on the art of horsemanship, Xenophon's *Hippike*, was written almost eight centuries before. This Greek commander had spent much of his time in battle and, as a result, saw many different styles of riding from various cultures, in the most practical of contexts. He advocated the use of stallions in warfare because they were thought to be braver, but disapproved of the bit, whip, and spur, characterizing their use as pure ignorance.

Xenophon's Principles

- The rider must understand the laws of gravity and principles of symmetry.

- The rider should adopt a centered and balanced riding position (classical seat).

- The rider must be patient and gentle, persuading the horse that each request was his idea in the first place.[3]

- A horse's agility can and should be improved through progressive exercises.

Roman equestrianism had much in common with the Greek tradition, particularly after the conquest of the latter state by the former empire in 146 BC. Like the Greeks, Roman horsemen adopted a classical seat, thereby creating engagement with the horse well back on his hocks. Both of these approaches were known for their lightness of hand in contrast to the firmer Germanic or Prussian styles.

During the Dark Ages, much of the beauty and grace of

---

3. "When your horse shies at an object and is unwilling to go up to it, he should be shown that there is nothing fearful in it, least of all to a courageous horse like himself."—Xenophon, *Hippike*.

classical horsemanship was eclipsed by the growing preference for heavily armored cold bloods (work horses)—more
the battleaxe than the rapier. Various technological break-
throughs contributed to the viability of the European medieval warhorse: the war saddle in the sixth century; the iron
stirrup and the curb bit in the seventh century; iron horse-
shoes in the ninth century; and spurs in the eleventh century.

As for the animal himself, beginning with the Arabian conquests of the seventh century, the tactical advantages of the
Middle Eastern hot bloods (horses bred to be fast and athletic) became increasingly evident. The age of Charlemagne
saw the decline of the Roman warhorse and the advent of
large, strong, but more agile, creatures produced by selective
breeding with Arabian stock. During the Crusades, European
nobles were again greatly struck by the speed and maneuver-
ability of these lighter horses. As a result, many such speci-
mens were imported into England and France. To this day, in
fact, all true thoroughbreds are thought to be the direct de-
scendants of these immigrants.

The combat utility of the warhorse also evolved in line with
technological innovations in the weaponry of the day. During
the age of heavy armor, the ironclad charger was employed
like a battering ram. With the advent of firearms and their
ability to penetrate even the heaviest of protective equipment, there was a resurgence of interest in the agility of a
lighter, more maneuverable mount. The *piaffe* and the flying
charge provided effective methods of advancing; the *levade*,
the *pirouette*, and the *courbette* were valuable close-quarters
battle skills; and the *capriole* afforded a means of escape over
low obstacles.[4]

---

4. These and many other tactical intricacies are more fully treated in Leslie A.
Neumann's excellent essay on the subject.

Federico Grisone's *The Rules of Horsemanship*, published in 1561, laid the foundation for the famous haute école of horsemanship, which Antoine de Pluvinel—riding instructor to Louis XIII—in turn employed as the basis for his *Instruction of the King in the Art of Mounting the Horse*. François Robichon de la Guérinière advocated a system for everyday riding that built on the principles of the haute école, and in 1733 published a seminal work on the subject entitled *School of Horsemanship*, which is still in use today in certain circles. De la Guérinière in particular advocated the adoption of a light hand so as not to injure the horse's mouth. William Cavendish, the Duke of Newcastle, served as riding instructor to King Charles II while they were both exiled in France. There he learned and built on the principles of the haute école, publishing *New Methods and Inventions for Training Horses* in 1658. Continuing in the humane tradition of Xenophon, Cavendish argued that the training of horses should be based on understanding and patience.

Common to most classical disciplines of horsemanship[5] is the premise that the rider is totally responsible for his horse. The noble beast agrees to forgo the liberty afforded to it in the state of nature, and in the case of the warhorse, it endures the pandemonium of battle; in exchange, the rider is obliged to care for his mount's needs and comfort and to assume full responsibility for the animal's training and performance. Care, breeding, and mastery of a warhorse required a substantial investment of money and time, and many died in combat. As a result, equestrian proficiency generally fell almost exclusively within the province of the noble houses. The complete education of a classical warrior has always been thought to

5. Sometimes referred to as dressage.

require at least a passing familiarity with the fundamentals of riding, in both the Western[6] and the Eastern[7] traditions. To this day, academies in Palermo, Saumur, Hannover, and Weedon instruct select members of their nations' armed forces in the art of horsemanship.

The Sword

The Japanese *katana* is primarily designed for cutting or more accurately, slicing, but thrusting techniques for the weapon are also taught. With respect to the rapier—the Western-edged weapon that has generated perhaps the most academic scrutiny—the reverse is true. The composition, structure, and reach of the rapier allow for the infliction of devastating puncture wounds, but the blade can still hold an edge. As a result of having witnessed the spectacle of modern fencing, a common misconception exists that European swords have always been flimsy tools employed in a flicking or rapping motion (perhaps more akin to *kendo* than *kenjutsu*). This is, generally speaking, an inaccurate supposition. The

6. Flatwork: maneuvering exercises for horse and rider.
7. *Yabusame*: the samurai art of shooting from horseback.

rapiers of the Renaissance were strong and heavy enough to inflict lethal injuries at a substantial distance using a variety of approaches while retaining unparalleled agility.

While samurai generally wore the katana with a companion sword, *wakizashi*, most styles of Japanese swordsmanship employed a two-handed grip, thereby negating the possibility of using both swords at once. Notable exceptions are the nito-ryu of warrior Miyamoto Musashi and its derivative styles.[8]

While these *ryu*, "martial traditions," generally embrace a certain number of two-sword techniques in their curricula, the emphasis tends to be on the ability to wield the katana with one hand as opposed to a sword in each. Similarly, while rapiers were exclusively single-handed weapons, they were often employed in conjunction with a main gauche, a shorter blade held in the left hand, and used to trap an opponent's blade in a fashion comparable to the Okinawan *sai* or Japanese *jutte*.[9] To the interested observer, the similarities between these particular styles of classical Japanese and European swordsmanship are evident as well as instructive.

In addition to its use as a medieval battlefield weapon, the European sword also enjoyed prominence as a dueling instrument. Even after the advent of firearms in the European theater, the blade retained a certain appeal as the weapon of choice on the field of honor. Similarly, even in the face of a ban on dueling with live blades in Japan, determined adversaries arranged to have "practice sessions" with wooden training swords. These encounters often generated lethal re-

---

8. For example the Hyoho and Santo Niten Ichi Ryu. Certain accounts also maintain that the legendary sword master Tsukuhara Bokuden wielded the katana *katate*, at least on occasion.
9. A method of fighting with two rapiers, the so-called Florentine style, also emerged in Renaissance Europe.

sults and gave rise to an entirely new style of combat known as *gekken*, "the severe sword."

In the same way that the martial traditions of the East became established and recognized on a national level, the Corporation of the Masters of the Noble Science of Defense, a British sword masters' guild, was established by Henry the VII in 1540. Its syllabus comprised several weapons systems and had four levels: scholar, free scholar, provost, and master. It was during this era that a number of seminal works, including Di Grassi's *His True Arte of Defence* and Saviolo's *his Practise: In Two Bookes*, were added to the written canon of the European art of the long sword.

As with the katana, the complexity of the tactical possibilities available to the rapier swordsman has caused much to be written on the use of such weapons. Two of the greatest master works on the subject of the cut-and-thrust sword,[10] *Paradoxes of Defence* and *Brief Instructions*, were written by Elizabethan master swordsman George Silver, at the end of the sixteenth century. Like any complete martial art, Silver's system also included the use of other weapons, such as the two-handed sword, the dagger, the staff, and the polearm, as well as various techniques of unarmed combat.

In the realm of the sciences, significant advances in Western metallurgical technology before and during the Renaissance allowed European sword makers to produce slender, flexible, high-carbon steel blades. At this time Japanese craftsmen had been following centuries-old, traditional forging methods in pursuit of similar qualities. In both cultures, the sword was thought to embody the soul of he who wielded it, and the honor of crafting such a weapon took on a religious quality.

By the early eighteenth century, the use of a smaller,

10. A close cousin of the rapier.

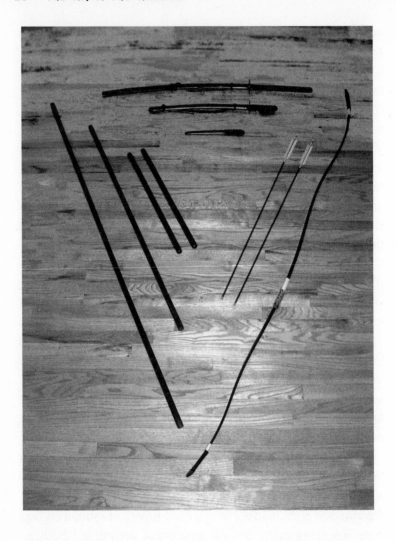

lighter, "court sword," had come into favor in European aris-
tocratic circles. It was the end of an era. From this pale
shadow of a former greatness, the modern sport of fencing
evolved. Just as modern kendo, with its reduction in emphasis on pure combat efficiency, displaced kenjutsu as the dom-
inant Japanese sword art in Japan, so the discipline of

classical European swordsmanship began its steady march into the history books. As with the classical arts of Japan, however, there remain a few traditionalists dedicated to the preservation of the true *Arte of Defence.*

The Empty Hand

Both Eastern and Western traditions agreed that training in the martial arts was an essential part of a noble education. Baldesar Castaglione's *Etiquette for Renaissance Gentlemen* teaches that "it is of the highest importance to know how to wrestle" as well as to display a thorough knowledge of horsemanship, weapons, and the tactics with which to employ them to best effect. Furthermore, in addition to instructing the combatant in the necessary technical skills of footwork, stances, attacks, evasions, and wards, many of the Western master texts, like their Asian counterparts, also dealt with more subtle considerations such as timing, distance, and judgment.

While many classical weapons schools augmented their existing curricula with the study of hand-to-hand combat, special mention should be made of those disciplines in European history that focused exclusively on methods of unarmed fighting. We know that the ancient Greeks introduced a fist art into their Olympic games in the seventh century BC, and that a reference to an early form of boxing even appears in the *Iliad*. Not satisfied with the sport's inherent violence, Roman pugilists contributed the *cestus*, "a leather hand strap, often reinforced with metal bands or studs," to the evolution of the art.

With the fall of the Roman Empire, formalized hand-to-hand combat had experienced a period of hibernation, but the efforts of such great fighters as James Figg and Jack Broughton revived it in eighteenth-century Britain. The bare-fist matches these men of iron endured were often bloody, sometimes lethal, and rarely encumbered by excessive regulation, at least until 1865 when John Chambers wrote a set of rules for the sport. This code was officially adopted two years later through the good offices of the Eighth Marquis of Queensbury, and under its provisions, James Corbett defeated the last of the great bare-knuckle fighters, John Sullivan, in 1892, marking the passing of another age.

The Marquis of Queensbury Rules

1. A fair stand-up boxing match, in a twenty-four foot ring.

2. No wrestling or clinching.

3. Three-minute rounds, one minute between rounds.

4. Ten seconds to rise and return to the scratch line.

5. A man hanging on the ropes in a helpless state is considered down.

6. No seconds or any other person allowed in the ring during the rounds.

7. If the match is stopped, the referee designates a time and place to continue.

8. The gloves must be fair-sized boxing gloves of the best quality, and new.

9. A glove that bursts, or comes off, must be replaced to the referee's satisfaction.

10. A man on one knee is considered down, and if struck, the other forfeits the match.

11. No shoes or boots with springs allowed.

12. In all other respects, the match is governed by the revised London Prize Ring rules.

Just as the touch system of modern fencing may be seen to lack a certain martial flavor, the methods and behavior of many modern exponents of the so-called sweet science detract considerably from boxing's status as an art. Nevertheless, the finer aspects of this classical tradition are still preserved through the efforts and teachings of a few, dedicated masters. There endure a number of boxers who seek to augment their abilities by studying the principles of stance, breathing, range, timing, and balance rather than simply resorting to the maladroit methodology of more powerful weapons and heavier armor.

The Sum of the Parts

No examination of the European martial tradition would be complete without reference to the peculiar characteristic that exemplifies the best qualities of the British nation at war—the ability to rise to the occasion. Perhaps a feature common to densely populated, ancient, island nations, Britain's military history is punctuated with examples of astounding victories by objectively inferior forces in defiance of all odds. Granted, these phenomena can often be explained as the result of superior strategy or technology or serendipity, but it would be foolish to deny that, at least on occasion, the whole really is greater than the sum of its parts.

Under the leadership of Prime Minister Winston Churchill, a beleaguered Britain fought off a powerful and malignant evil during World War II, alone for a time and armed with little more than ingenuity, determination, and grit. British forces refused to yield at sea, in the air, and on the land and acquitted themselves with distinction and valor and, above all, in strict observance of the laws of war. In May 1940, with the German invasion of France, Allied troops were driven back to the coast of France into the town of Dunkirk. Beginning on May 26, an armada of British ships, from Royal Navy vessels to fishing boats, with support from the Royal Air Force, rescued 300,000 troops from the clutches of the enemy.

The Allied withdrawal from the continent, however, left only the Channel between the English homeland and the grasp of the Axis powers. In July 1940, during the Battle of Britain, the vastly superior forces of the Luftwaffe, under the command of Hermann Göring, were held at bay by the Royal Air Force, and a German invasion of England was averted, even though the defenders were desperately short of planes, parts, and pilots. "This," according to Churchill, "was their finest hour." On September 7, 1940, Germany began the unrestricted bombing of London. The British people, Churchill assured the Axis powers, would never surrender. They would choose to stand fast, and mete out the measure—and more than the measure—that had been meted out to them.

Great Britain did indeed endure, and on June 6, 1944, Operation Overlord was launched. Allied forces stormed the beaches of Normandy, straight into the teeth of well-entrenched enemy defenses, retaking occupied territory through sheer force of will. The operation succeeded in driving back the Nazi menace, and on May 8, 1945, Victory in Europe Day, the unconditional surrender of the principle Axis power was achieved. The V for victory sign can still be seen faintly painted on the walls of King's College Cambridge. It is said that the British always win at least one battle—the last. Add this to the historical record of the English martial tradition.

5. *SHOSHIN* — AN OPEN MIND

A young branch takes on all the bends that one gives it

—*Penjing* teaching

The master leaned on his four-foot walking stick and pulled thoughtfully on his pipe. At length, he drew himself up, raised the tip of his staff, and indicated a particular blossom hanging precariously from the tip of a high branch of the ancient cherry tree. It was about seven feet above the ground. "Kick," he commanded. The target was obviously too high, especially for an aspirant who had never kicked at anything taller than a football in his life. The master met the young one's apparent hesitation with a frown. After a moment, the prospective student tried and then fell flat on his back. The blossom continued to flutter in the breeze, unscathed. "This will take time," the master said, muttering to himself. The student fumed. Surely, any good teacher would have known that a novice could never hope to have performed such a technique. Many years later, the master explained, "It was not to see if you could kick the leaf that I asked. It was to see if you would try."

Students who apply for acceptance into a classical system of martial arts stand at the threshold of a tradition that extends back many millennia and reaches to the farthest corners of the earth. They are not merely seeking admission into a dojo, but into ryu. There are many places for studying the martial arts. There are schools, academies, clubs, teams, temples, and backyards. But long before such institutions were established, there was ryu.

In ancient times, teachings were passed from father to son, from *sempai* to *kohai*, from master to student, and from samurai to apprentice in an unending chain. The character for ryu denotes flowing, as water. It captures perfectly the concept of the direct, personal transmission of an art, which is precisely what sets ryu apart from less traditional methods of instruction. Ryu is as far removed from modern forms of institutional instruction as handcrafting is from mass production. In deciding to accept an individual into a ryu, the teacher is welcoming the student on behalf of all those who have gone before. This decision is an important one. It is based not on strength, ability, or preexisting skill. These things can be taught. It is based on spirit, attitude, and character. These things can only be cultivated. For this reason, some say the white belt is the most important rank of all.

The ancient story is told of the young hopeful who went to see a famous teacher, seeking to be accepted as a student. The two sat down to talk over tea. The young one was full of ideas and suggestions. Without saying a word, the teacher began pouring more tea into his guest's already brimming cup, spilling it all over the floor. "Why do you do this, can you not see that the cup is already full!" the visitor asked? "Like this cup," the host replied, "your mind is also full. You must empty it before we can begin."

Does this mean students should have no thoughts of their own? That they must never ask questions of the teacher? No. It simply means that in the context of ryu, students will be exposed to theories, techniques, and methods battle tested by centuries of application and passed directly from *sensei* to *deshi*. These teachings may seem fruitless or impossible at first. They are hard to apply. They are even more difficult to master. Students must trust in them. They must trust in the teacher. They must trust in their fellow students. They must trust in themselves because each has proven worthy to be accepted into the ryu. This willingness to accept the wisdom of something wholly beyond one's current comprehension is known as *shoshin*, "beginning mind."

It is said that when the student is ready, the master will appear. Mastery is all around us, in the back alleys of Chinatown, in the basement dojo where two or three gather, in the late evening sessions at the university gymnasium, or in the secluded corner of the botanical garden where the grass is as soft as *tatami*. But until we have opened our minds to new possibilities, it remains a shadow in the twilight and a whisper on the autumn breeze.

6. *JUNSHIN* — A PURE HEART

And now here is my secret, a very simple secret; it is
only with the heart that one can see rightly; what is
essential is invisible to the eye.

—Antoine de Saint-Exupéry

Many traditional ryu require the student to execute *keppan*
upon admission. Others require a written petition outlining
the candidate's motivation in seeking instruction. Historically
speaking, this was no mere formality; for once an apprentice
was accepted into a certain dojo, the master explained, the
teacher became responsible for the new student's future conduct. Thus, it was of paramount importance to judge wisely
the aspirant's character, for self-serving as well as altruistic
reasons.

Attempting to predict with specificity the way in which a
person will react to a given situation is an exercise in futility.

Worse still is the misguided attempt to program into the student a set of conditioned responses to every conceivable occurrence. It discourages original thought and is eventually destined to fail. The master's approach was to introduce an idea or principle and then trust that the apprentice would be able to apply that teaching to any situation in which it was appropriate to do so. In this way, he did not look primarily for wisdom, righteousness, or good judgment in his students. He looked for a pure heart. The rest, he said, would follow as a matter of course.

The difficulty here is that one cannot see purity of the heart with the eyes. It must be sensed as one recognizes the presence of a kindred spirit. How many times does a person observe some social nicety—perhaps the holding of a door, the offering of some minor generosity, or the expressing of a deferential sentiment—only to have the other plow past it, oblivious to its very existence? These people, according to the master's teachings, are to be pitied, for they rarely raise their snouts from the trough long enough to appreciate the subtlety of the world that exists just beyond the ambit of their limited perception.

Then there are those who simply accept such noble tendencies in others without any thought of reciprocity, seeing them as a convenient peculiarity. These people are to be avoided, for they are the parasites who drain the lifeblood from a code of conduct and a *modus vivendi* already on the brink of extinction. Finally, there are those who reject such ways entirely, actively embracing an egocentric, grasping, and adversarial approach to life. These people are to be watched closely, for they are the ones with whom the warrior is most likely to have to do battle. However impressive the walls such people have erected around their position may be, their defenses must eventually collapse, for they have no foundation.

Purity of heart is a hard way. It promises no payoff, at least in any pragmatic sense of the term. It does not make sense from a cost-benefit point of view. It is not lucrative, glamorous, or often even enjoyable. It can drain rather than supplement one's resources. It is likely to make the adherent less popular, at least with the majority, not more. It will certainly cut into one's free time. It is the impulse to clean up litter you did not leave; to befriend the one whom no one else will; to pay a bill that is not your own; and to take the time to talk with a friend or acquaintance in need on the telephone or in person, when you would much rather be doing something else.

For every one such idealist, there are legions of realists or pragmatists or egotists or worse. The pure of heart are therefore likely to remain unidentified, underappreciated, and exploited the vast majority of the time. But once in a very great while, perhaps in one of a thousand encounters, there will come a fellow traveler. Like émigrés reunited in a distant land, an enduring bond will form. An instantaneous understanding will take hold. And a kinship that can rarely be broken will quicken. The master was such a one.

7. *FUDOSHIN*—A DETERMINED SPIRIT

But I am constant as the Northern Star/Of whose true
and resting quality/There is no fellow in the firmament.

—*Julius Caesar*, Act III, Scene I

When asked whether his own teacher had ever been beaten
in single combat, the master reflected upon the question for a
moment, as he was wont to do. Then he replied, "Bested, yes,
beaten, no." There is a difference. There are few things over
which a person can exercise absolute control in life. Will is
one. We might wish to be wiser, stronger, quicker, or more
agile than we are, all to no avail, but determination falls entirely within the realm of our own power. Defeat is a competitive phenomenon. Surrender is a unilateral decision.

The martial way is often steep and the path difficult to
tread. Those who sprint at the beginning are likely to run out

of breath or turn an ankle midcourse. Obstacles can loom large, and even the dedicated traveler will inevitably reach *daichi* and a place and time where progress seems imperceptible and further effort, fruitless. Precisely at such times *fudoshin*, "an immovable spirit," either emerges or does not. Teachers of all kinds strive to test their students' resolve, pushing them into precisely this frustrated frame of mind in microcosm or simulation, to forge and temper their will.

Professors set scholars to the translation or analysis of impossibly advanced subject matter. Drill sergeants deprive recruits of sleep as well as rest. Outward Bound instructors send candidates into the wilderness without food or shelter. Flight instructors cut the power to both engines on takeoff. Dive masters turn off the oxygen valve at depth. In the martial arts, these boundaries are tested in *shugyo*. Such spirit forging can take many forms.

There is *tanren*—prolonged exercise under severe circumstances: extreme heat, cold, or other conditions. There is *kata*—the exact performance of a series of precise techniques over a shorter period of time, where any significant error results in failure. Then there is *shiai*—competition against one or several opponents, the number of whom and duration of which increases until the very limit of the fighter's ability is reached. Such practices may seem harsh and should certainly be tempered with a healthy dose of common sense, but they all proceed from a fundamentally constructive proposition: Testing the student's abilities among colleagues and under the watchful eye of an experienced teacher is better than in the hostile and unpredictable medium of a real-life challenge.

The student is not expected to pass these tests flawlessly or even with any great degree of finesse. In fact, the very purpose is to push the examinee past the ability to perform with poise, to strip away the defensive armor, and to gauge the quality of the material beneath it.

Two things, however, are expected of the unfortunate subject of these exercises: The first is that the student must retain his composure. Once anger, frustration, embarrassment, or pain are allowed to well up to the surface, the battle is lost. Self-control must be maintained at all times, even in defeat. The second is that while the student may evade, retreat, or even concede under some circumstances, he must not quit. He must not allow himself to be beaten. Like Robert the Bruce's apocryphal spider, he must try, try, and try again. To concede is an active measure. To be beaten is passive. You will not find honor in collapsing on the field; dropping to one's knee to gather breath and strength for the riposte is another matter altogether. You can tell from the glint in the eye.

8. *IHTARAM* — A CIVIL CODE

When you have to kill a man it costs nothing to be polite.

—Sir Winston Churchill

Gichin Funakoshi, the acknowledged father of Okinawan *te*, is reputed to have articulated the principle that there is no first attack in karate. This sentiment has been construed by many in a philosophical sense to the effect that it is morally wrong to initiate conflict. If this were the extent of his teaching, it would be a laudable and worthy decree. Yet one of the accepted interpretations of the meaning of the Okinawan kata, known as thirteen hands, is that the first eight moves are defensive in nature, whereas the latter five are offensive. Certainly, anyone who has practiced this form will appreciate the aggressive nature of its latter portion.

A slight semantic distinction in the translation of Funakoshi's edict may, in part, explain this apparent inconsistency. The master said, "There is no *advantage* in the first attack." Lessons learned in sparring support the proposition that it is often easier to score on an opponent in response to an attack than it is to penetrate a stable, defensive posture. The fraction of the opponent's attention and arsenal committed to an offensive action is unavailable, at least momentarily, for defensive purposes. The counterattack, therefore, has a greater probability of succeeding. Rather than adopting this explanation as an alternative to the ethical version of Funakoshi's maxim, it should simply be regarded as the pragmatic counterpart to the nobler interpretation.

Similarly, most practitioners of the martial arts are familiar with the saying that karate begins and ends with respect. There is clearly value in teaching courtesy to students of the martial arts for courtesy's sake alone, especially in an age when principles of etiquette are virtual anachronisms. But this expression embraces a deeper meaning as well. The civil code common to many martial cultures derives from practical as well as idealistic sources. The complex hierarchy governing ancient Japanese society depended, in large part, on strict observance of many customs appropriate to the relative rank of the parties to any given transaction. To lose face, especially because of a deliberate insult, was considered a matter of great dishonor and could often give rise to lethal consequences. The observance of proper courtesy—literally courtly behavior—was a vital skill for the samurai, and much of the *reishiki* seen in *koryu bujutsu* is a modern manifestation of this ancient necessity. Similarly, the throwing of the gauntlet in the European tradition was generally followed by further discussion of the matter on the field of combat at dawn the next day.

The need for a civil code derives not only from the interaction of people, which of course occurs within the artificial

construct of a given society but also from the natural environment within which that society functions. Common to many
harsh climes, for example, is the unwritten rule that refuge
shall be given to any traveler seeking it. It was this tradition
that allowed the Campbell assassins to take advantage of the
hospitality of the MacDonald Clan, in the barren highlands of
Glencoe, and then to murder their sleeping hosts in the wee
hours of February 13, 1692.

The *Rub' al Khali*, Saudi Arabia's so-called Empty Quarter,
has been described as the most desolate and forbidding place
on the surface of the planet: sand dunes tower over a thousand
feet, daytime temperatures can exceed 120 degrees Fahren-
heit, and nighttime temperatures often plummet to minus 32.
Only bandits and experienced travelers dare venture into
even its outermost boundaries. As a result, among the indigenous Bedouin, etiquette requires that shelter be given to any
person who asks. According to the code, the traveler is to be
muhtaram, "the recipient of respect."

The story is told around the campfire late at night, after the
children have been put to bed and the wives have retired, of
the bandit who came upon the camp of a Bedouin chieftain.
The chieftain invited the other man into his home, as custom
dictated, and offered him tea. The traveler accepted immediately, thereby betraying his true nature, for an Arabian gentleman is required initially to refuse what is offered to him,
accepting only after the third or fourth entreaty. In this way,
even a poor man can still offer hospitality once or twice, as
the code requires, without actually having to provide it, in the
event that he cannot afford to do so.

As the evening wore on, the host's generosity was equaled
only by his guest's bad manners. The visitor took far more
than his share of the meager rations. He treated the family
and servants harshly. The greater the courtesy extended to

him, it seemed, the more his greed and arrogance grew. After the chieftain had finally fallen asleep on his cushion in the dining room (for it would have been inexcusable to abandon his guest, who seemed to be enjoying himself tremendously), the brigand went to the bedchamber, where he attacked one of his host's wives and killed his eldest son for trying to intervene. Awakened by the commotion, the chieftain demanded to know what had happened. A tearful servant relayed the details of the crime, and proffered his master's scimitar.[11]

The chieftain shook his head sadly and merely ordered the servant to ensure that their guest wanted for nothing during the course of the night. Just before sunrise the following day, the bandit awoke and presented himself in the kitchen. He demanded to be fed and to be provided rations for the rest of his trip. The chieftain simply nodded his assent. The outlaw rode from the compound at first light, unscathed, saddlebags heavy with treasures plundered from his host. The code had been observed. Tradition upheld. The obligation completed. It was not until he was well beyond the boundaries of the chieftain's lands that the bandit became aware that he was not alone. The scimitar flickered and flashed in the unforgiving morning sun.

While societal convention is no longer as rigid and nature rarely as inhospitable for the modern warrior, the observance of courtesy is still important. Any serious study of the martial arts carries with it the inherent dangers of a contact sport, aggravated by the adversarial or, at least competitive, paradigm

11. The scimitar is the elegant, curved blade of the Bedouin warrior. The story is told of Richard Coeur de Lion's first meeting with Saladin at the beginning of the Crusades. It is said that Richard drew his broadsword and brought it splintering down on a nearby table in a symbolic gesture of the resolve of the English. In response, Saladin tossed a silk handkerchief into the air, and as it floated down gently onto the edge of his upturned scimitar, it was sliced in two.

that generally emerges in such training. The best and surest way to avoid accidental injury or ill-considered action, either within or without the dojo walls, is to observe the principles of etiquette and the values of courtesy at all times. Trained fighters, much more than average people, have an obligation to employ their skills judiciously, to govern themselves and their emotions at all times, to follow the code, and to begin and end with respect.

9. *ENKYOKU* — THE WINDING WAY

To travel hopefully is a better thing than to arrive, and
the true success is to labor.

—Robert Louis Stevenson

Almost every style of the martial arts has a symbol: the
Shotokan tiger, the *Daito Ryu* diamond, the Okinawan *mitsu-
tomoe*, "triple tear shape." It is even said that the essence of
some arts can be represented symbolically. For example, the
gentle blending of many styles of *aikido* may be seen as a circle, whereas the straight blast of the *Itto Ryu* might be best
represented by a sharp line.

The *Meditations* of Marcus Aurelius exhort, "Make for thy-
self a definition or description of the thing which is presented
to thee, so as to see distinctly what kind of a thing it is in its
substance, in its nudity, in its complete entirety, and tell thy-
self its proper name, and the names of the things of which it

has been compounded, and into which it will be resolved."
Kishido is, in its substance, its entirety, and its eventual reso-
lution, indirect in nature.

In the Japanese language, the master explained, to employ
the second person pronoun in conversation is considered
gauche. It is akin to pointing a finger at someone. It is considered more polite, for example, to inquire in general, "Is there
hunger?" Traditional British culture mirrors this oblique approach to interpersonal dynamics. Comments are deliberately
left vague and necessary inquiries or assertions couched in
euphemism and elaborate circumlocution. It is, perhaps, another evolutionary development necessary to the dynamics
of densely populated island societies. For this reason, the
uneri symbol of Kishido is particularly apt, and, like any useful symbol, the permutations of its meaning are potentially
infinite.

By modern standards, the shortest distance between two
points is, indeed, a straight line. But this axiom presupposes
that the goal is to reach one's destination by the shortest
available path. Applying this principle to the odyssey of life
would have us all hurtling toward the grave by the most direct

route—sadly, not an altogether unprecedented phenomenon in the modern era. The sage tells us that there are many routes to the mountaintop. The direct approach is an immediate bid for the summit across the shortest face. Consider, for a moment, another way: a thorough reconnoiter of the foothills, assessing the obstacles and test pieces; a staged, expedition-style initial ascent, allowing for exploration of a variety of faces; the unplanned decisions to go bivouacking from time to time, absorbing the serenity of the place; the occasional glissade, doing it just for fun; and the eventual summit when the time is right, and not before. This is, of course, not the only way. It is merely a way worth considering, and it requires patience and persistence. This is the indirect route.

Furthermore, while the winding way certainly covers more ground, it may also prove the more expedient path on occasion. For example, when the air is streaming over the quarterdeck, sailing a so-called broad reach will deliver one's maritime destination more quickly than simply running with the wind astern. While it may seem counterintuitive, the additional speed derived from rigging the sails in this fashion and charting a zigzag path to best harness the prevailing winds more than compensates for the greater distance covered.

In the martial realm, the indirect way gives rise to five fundamental principles: misdirection, reversal, alternation, insinuation, and continuity. Each of these *genri* in turn, gives rise to strategies (*heiho*); strategies to tactics (*giho*); and tactics to techniques (*waza*). For example, the principle of misdirection is based on the notion that the adversary may be quicker than one may be. A full frontal assault is, therefore, not to be favored. A resulting stratagem, depending on the circumstances, might therefore be, "Knock at one gate, enter another." A tactical manifestation of this stratagem might be to lure the opponent's defenses high and to his left with a feint, only to strike at a lower target on his right side. The appropriate technique, in turn, might well be *sakibouchi*, "the cat's paw strike." This is but one possible application of the martial progression derived from *enkyoku*.

10. *GANSHIKI* — INSIGHT

The gaze should be large and broad. This is the
twofold gaze—perception and sight. Perception is
strong and sight weak.

—Miyamoto Musashi

The master said that one should expect no praise merely for
the performance of one's duty. Working in an office, at a
trade, or as a parent is part of what is expected. It is *giri*,
"one's duty." The measure of a person, according to the master's school of thought, begins at the conclusion of mandatory
obligations and encompasses the extracurricular, the voluntary, and the philanthropic. The samurai maxim tells us that
giri is heavier than a mountain, death, lighter than a feather.
The observance of giri, therefore, is not optional. The minimum is acceptable conduct. According to Admiral Lord Nelson,
it is what England expects of every man. As a result, it tells us

very little about a person, beyond the fact that he will do at least what is required.

Ninjo, "one's true desire," on the other hand, speaks volumes. What one chooses to think and do and say after the indispensable tasks have been completed has the most profound effect on the forging of character. Likewise, the greatest insights are often achieved not in the office, the classroom, or the dojo, but in the bath, the kitchen, and that twilight realm between bed and sleep. Accordingly, relegating one's studies or practices to a particular place and time in an effort to compartmentalize one's life is counter productive. Musashi tells us that our combat spirit should be our everyday spirit. While it may be tidier to cordon off discrete subjects one from the other, it prevents the possibility of blending, analogizing, and thinking laterally—the primordial sludge of ingenuity.

Therefore, one must maintain an appropriate balance between the concrete, obligatory, objective constraints of the outside world and the abstract, whimsical subjectivity of one's inner universe. One may have to endure the ennui of a tedious job day after day, but no factory is so dismal that it can block in an active imagination, no jail cell so secure that it can blot out the starlight. Even if surrounded by stunted, myopic intellects, one can still commune with the ancient masters through their works. The mind must be kept active, inquisitive, and agile. The master says that if you cannot deduce five facts about someone simply by the way he enters a room, you are clearly not paying attention.

In the context of any martial training, clearly the emphasis is on discipline, obedience, and order. These external behaviors must, of course, be observed scrupulously. It may be tempting, as a result, to disengage one's unpredictable inner faculties as well—to function as some sort of unquestioning automaton. This is a misguided way as well as a terrible waste of the gift of individuality.

The British Special Air Service (SAS), one of the most well-respected unconventional warfare forces in the world, was the brainchild of Captain David Stirling, a Scots Guard, and Jock Lewes, an officer with the Welsh Guards. In the latter years of World War II, the regiment took an altogether novel approach to combat in the North African theater, based, in part, on the idea that a soldier should be able to function independently of his command structure if necessary. Its founders had seen entire platoons disabled by the loss of their commanding officers in combat, and they aimed to create a better type of soldier—one who could operate effectively both as an individual and as a member of a team. As a result, to this day, SAS soldiers enjoy discretion with respect to their appearance, equipment, and training, to a degree unheard of in other military units, and intended, at least in part, to nurture in them a degree of autonomy.[12]

In the dojo, the student must, of course, follow the teacher's instructions without hesitation or debate, but not without thought or subsequent consideration. Granted, some principles must be taken on faith, at least for a period of time, until repeated practice reveals their true nature, but everything the student is taught should be examined, assessed, and tested before being fully accepted as truth. Similarly, the teacher must give consistent instruction and set fixed goals, to maintain both the standards of the tradition and the caliber of the deshi. It would be foolish, however, to ignore the

---

12. It is virtually impossible, for example, to teach a drill-hardened soldier to walk or talk like a civilian again.

existence of individual strengths and weaknesses; a waste of potential and a pedagogical failing. While all students should be taught proficiency in the core skills of the art, the weight lifter's curriculum should vary from the ballerina's significantly.

Both teacher and student must see beyond the exterior of things or, *omote*. This is the twofold gaze: sight and perception. Those who use their artistic talents merely to reproduce the great works of past masters are known as forgers. Within the rigid boundaries of the frame, each painting should be different, and both the educator and the educated are responsible for preserving that individuality. To penetrate the heart of a matter, according to the master, you must see far. To do so, you must look deeply.

11. *DISCRETIO MATER VIRTUTIS—* RESTRAINT

You are educated when you have the ability to listen to almost anything without losing your temper or self-confidence.

—Robert Frost

Anger, according to the master, is merely a manifestation of fear. It is like the snarling of a frightened beast. It serves no useful purpose in combat other than, perhaps, on the rare occasions when such posturing works to frighten an adversary away. But such conduct will deter only the most fainthearted and, therefore, least dangerous of opponents. To paraphrase President John Kennedy: Only when our arms are sufficient without doubt, can we be certain without doubt that they will rarely have to be employed, and, thus, behave accordingly.

The master would sometimes tell of the so-called parking lot brawls commonly employed during his youth to resolve severe differences of opinion in the martial community. He would hasten to add that this was not the modern way and was to be avoided whenever possible. But when pressed for details, he would describe how two rivals would sometimes reach an impasse, and if the point were sufficiently important to both, a meeting would be arranged outside the training hall to test their competing positions (for to degrade the sanctity of the dojo with such rancor would be unforgivable).

There was little bluster or bravado involved in this process. The presence of the opponents at the appointed place was sufficient indication of their resolve. Even on the brink of single combat, the adversaries would typically conduct themselves with a full measure of dignity. When telling these stories, however, the master was always careful to add that to exercise restraint was of course better before arriving at such a state of affairs, but, alas, this was not always possible. When confronted with an unyielding and unacceptable affront, action had to be taken. One must try to avoid such situations, but never to shrink from them.

Contrast the dynamic of these historic duels—calmly and quietly staking one's reputation on a physical and psychological contest—with the shrill and venomous invective that often characterizes modern debate. All too often in the courtroom, on television, and in the Internet forums of today, self-important armchair warriors swagger and strut, safely removed from the possibility of having to defend their positions with anything more substantial than misspelled prose and tortured grammar. The master commands that we reject this practice. No matter how tempting it might be to interrupt a misguided conversation or to weigh in on an adversarial chat page, walk away. The tenor of such hollow squabbling cheapens the subject and the speaker. Exercise restraint. Just walk away.

Despite one's best efforts to the contrary, an encounter with a determined troublemaker will invariably present itself from time to time along the way. This type of scenario is what the wide-eyed neophyte has in mind when asking if the teacher has ever had to "use" his martial training. The answer is generally yes, but not in the way that the student has in mind. The seasoned martial artist can usually recognize the presence of another warrior immediately, and while noncombatants are generally accorded an equal measure of deference, they are not shaped for warfare. As a result, their outbursts are akin to the barking of a dog and should be accorded as much attention.

By way of example, the tale is told of the martial arts master who, in his later years, became accustomed to taking the train from his country estate to his dojo in the city. On one such occasion, the tranquility of the late afternoon ride was disrupted by the arrival of an unruly young man, who, quite clearly intoxicated, was accosting various passengers, intent on a fight. Immediately concerned for the well-being and comfort of his fellow passengers, this master rose from his seat and addressed himself to the drunk. Rather than commanding the man to sit down and be quiet, he simply said, "You seem upset, my friend. Come sit with me, and we will talk about it."

Caught rather off guard and unwilling to stand down at the behest of a man twice his age, the young one lurched menacingly toward the master, muttering obscenities. Onlookers, familiar with the elder's reputation, held their breath in anticipation of the imminent clash. None came. Neither advancing nor flinching, the master simply held his ground, locking his gaze with the other's. His expression betrayed no fear, for his heart harbored none. Inches from the master's position, eyewitnesses reported, the would-be attacker halted his progress and dissolved into tears. The master then embraced the man, and, through racking sobs, patiently listened to the litany of disasters that had befallen the young one, thereby reducing him to his present state.

When the threat is real, imminent, and unswerving, however (an occurrence that is generally occasioned by less fanfare rather than more), the appropriate response is quiet resolve. This will immediately make it clear that the stakes are quite high and the time for bluffing has ended. It will also allow the practitioner to retain sufficient composure to defuse the situation if possible or to withdraw without surrender. Should the scenario deteriorate even further, the preferable way is to approach hostilities with Drake's legendary *sangfroid* and demonstrate restraint at all times. This, according to the master, is appropriate to the Way of the Western Warrior.

12. *NOBLESSE OBLIGE*—OBLIGATION

From him to whom much is given, shall much be expected.

—Gospel of Saint Luke

The master lived in a monastery for a season. For as long as anyone could remember, the grounds of that place had been tended by a dwarf who lived in a nearby cottage. The owner of the land on which the cottage stood decided that he no longer wanted the dwarf and his pregnant wife as tenants. So one frosty winter day, he summarily notified them that they were to be evicted. In the monastery, the master became aware of the growing commotion and intervened to offer his services as a translator, for the dwarf spoke in a peculiar rural dialect. At length, the master's temperance was overborne by the arrogance and cruelty of the landlord. He struck him once, but not very hard. The landlord crumpled. The master

fixed his withering gaze on the opponent. There was no response. The novices looking on from a high window cheered.
To their way of thinking, this episode was the manifestation
of the noble obligation the master taught them—championing
the defenseless and oppressed. It was certainly a moment of
high drama.

Several weeks later, the students were somewhat less im-
pressed with the result. The landowner, of course, had a legal
right, however heartless, to evict the diminutive groundskeeper
and his family. The master, on the other hand, had committed
himself fully to their cause. The line for the bathroom in the
morning was now even longer. The endless crying disturbed
previously sound sleep. And for several months, the whole
monastery smelled of new baby. It was this price and not the
cost of combat with which the master had satisfied the debt of
obligation.

When promoting to a teaching rank, some sensei will give
the student the gift of a stone. It is said to symbolize the burden, the *on*, that has now passed to the graduate. Whether or
not this paradigm is made explicit through such symbolism,
one must understand that every ability, innate or learned,
carries with it a corresponding obligation. It is not required by
constitution or statute. It is not defined by regulation or man-
ual. It exists nonetheless, and it derives from *ius cogens*, "a
more compelling source of law."

Like purity of heart, honoring noblesse oblige is rarely
prestigious, relaxing, or profitable. It can, in fact, play havoc
with one's schedule and finances. It is, however, an integral
part of any true way, a fact that should be considered carefully before taking up such a burden.

PART TWO

Range

13. *BANGEI* — VERSATILITY

A single arrow is easily broken, but not ten in a
bundle.

—Japanese proverb

Musashi instructs that the warrior should become ac-
quainted with every art and know the way of all professions.
We live, however, in an age of increasing specialization. In
law and medicine, the trend is away from general practice.
The value of a liberal arts education has been eclipsed by the
appeal of more lucrative majors. The assembly line approach
dominates. The doctor cannot prepare his own tax return.
The accountant is incapable of hunting or even cooking his
food. The lawyer has neither the skill nor the inclination to

perform a simple oil change. And virtually no one can write an adequate letter.

To take the winding way, studying the rudiments of the arts and sciences, as well as learning myriad practical skills, is neither expedient nor profitable. One can survive in the modern world largely by relying on the abilities of others. If something hurts, go to the doctor. If something annoys you, see your lawyer. If you are hungry, go to the supermarket or, if the culinary arts also elude you, the take-out window. For some, however, mere survival is not enough. While it is certainly valuable to be the master of at least one trade, a few strive to be jacks of all, or at least several. They thirst for life, in its infinite diversity.

His Royal Highness the Duke of Edinburgh, seeing the wisdom of this approach, founded an award scheme in 1956 for the classic all-rounder. This international program embraces athletic and academic achievement as well as the spirit of exploration and community service. Award winners have gone on to reach the summit of their particular mountains in all walks of life, but perhaps more importantly, they have followed more than one path in their ascent. They have achieved breadth as well as depth.

Some martial artists insist that theirs is the only way, forbidding students to cross-train under any circumstances. Worse still are those who actively degrade the teachings of other traditions, in an effort to justify their own narrow view. To close the mind to possibility is a tragic waste. To preach this philosophy to others is a violation of the sacred trust that has been placed in them as teachers.

To his great credit, the master always welcomed the influence of other arts, seeking to synthesize rather than to compete. Despite the comprehensiveness of his system and the profundity of his skill, he remained open to the notion that fresh ideas could often be integrated and new lessons learned. In this way, he imbued his teachings with an organic quality that would continue to thrive long after his own time had passed.

To insist that the master's way is inherently superior would be to violate this very tenet of his philosophy. The single-minded dedication of those who choose to walk but one path is to be admired, and their contentment, envied, for the benefits of that way are apparent. But theirs is another book. This is the way of the winding path. Its rewards are obscure. Perhaps, in the end, as the adage instructs, the finest purpose of a liberal education is simply to make one's mind a pleasant place to spend one's leisure.

14. *BUNBUICHI*—SWORD AND BRUSH

Though Bushido naturally implies first of all the qualities of strength and forcefulness, to have this one side only developed is to be nothing but a rustic samurai of no great account. . . . A samurai should take up verse making or study tea ceremony . . . for if he does not study he will not be able to understand the reason of things either past or present.

—Daidoji Yuzan

One day the master asked a young student to lead the class through *taiso*. The young one hesitated, afraid that she might forget the exact order of the stretches. "It is simple," he reminded her. "Begin with the first exercise, and work your way down the body. Which part do we stretch first?"

One of the senior students, more accustomed to the typical class format said, "The neck."

Before the master could reply, the young one said, "No sensei, we begin by stretching the mind." The master merely smiled. *"Mokuso,"* the student announced, and the class began the meditation ceremony.

In the midst of a passage discussing the resolute acceptance of death in the way of the warrior, Tsunetomo Yamamoto's *Hagakure* mentions the importance of *shodo,* "calligraphy." Legend has it that a four-eyed man named *Tsangh-hsieh* was the first to engage in the practice of character drawing in the third millennium BC. It is said that he was inspired by the tracks of passing animals. More scholarly sources place the origin of calligraphy in the East during the *Shang* period (second millennium BC) as evidenced by engravings found on tortoise shells dating back to that era. In any event, this system of writing kanji (literally: Chinese characters) was imported by the Japanese around the fifth century AD, and refined as an art form over the centuries that followed.

Particularly during the Heian period, a time of relative peace in Japanese history, samurai culture experienced a kind of renaissance. Relieved of the call of battle for a time and influenced by the influx of Buddhist practices from points west, the warrior class had an opportunity to delve into more pacific pursuits, and it was certainly in the Shogun's interest to encourage this type of diversion. So successful was the fusion of physical and cerebral practices that some classical treatises refer to shodo as the seventh martial art.

Whatever its genesis, this approach to a rounded martial education produces warriors who are truly armed at all points. The delicate balance follows the cosmological law of in and yo, yin and yang, balancing soft with hard, light with dark, and construction with destruction. Moreover, it is said that from one thing, you can know ten-thousand things. The strokes of the character *ei*, fundamental to the practice of shodo, are analogous to those of kenjutsu's *happogiri*, "the eight cuts." The principles of *feng shui* are similar to the directional precepts of the internal Chinese martial arts. And the nurture and care of *bonsai* is similar in many ways to the propagation of students.

While gaining an appreciation for a variety of subjects is an unavoidable side effect of taking the indirect path, it is also an important part of the intended destination. In addition to contributing to the production of a well-rounded character, the study of one or some of these nonmartial arts can teach patience and attention to detail as well as fostering an appreciation of subtlety, serenity, and style.

15. *BOKUDEN, IMA!*—
ANACHRONISM?

If you know the enemy and know yourself, you need
not fear the result of a hundred battles. If you know
yourself but not the enemy, for every victory gained
you will also suffer a defeat. If you know neither the
enemy nor yourself, you will succumb in every battle.

—Sun Tzu

In 1930, an article appeared in the Japanese press entitled
"Bokuden, Ima!" In it, the author drew a parallel between
Takeda Sogaku, the then headmaster of the Daito Ryu, and
the legendary sixteenth-century swordsman Tsukahara Bokuden. Bokuden is considered by many to represent the ultimate fusion of the arts of war and peace—a superb warrior
whose prowess on the battlefield was equaled only by his lyri-
cal artistry. His poetry can be explored in a collection known

as *Bokuden Ikun Sho*. Three hundred years later, Takeda is said to have wandered from dojo to dojo, challenging all comers and always emerging victorious. On the road to Sendai in 1882, it is said that he killed a number of attackers who were foolish enough to pick a fight with him. Even as recently as the master's youth, duels in the form of training accidents were not uncommon.

There is much to recommend valiant attempts to preserve many of the ancient ways. The Way of the Western Warrior, in fact, is dedicated to this principle. But we no longer live in the seventeenth century or even the twentieth. Sun Tzu's seminal treatise on war dedicates two full chapters to the importance of knowing one's environment and deploying one's assets accordingly. The enlightened warrior must therefore take into account modern innovations and societal conventions in the formulation of strategy. To do otherwise is to fail as a strategist.

Among the more significant differences in the modern era is the technology of weaponry. In ancient times, one would train for years, often decades, in order to master the bow, the sword, or the staff. Today one can acquire a firearm and use it to devastating effect with less effort than it takes to complete a single class in a classical weapons system. This development has had the effect of distancing the person from the act, with horrific consequences. The discipline, the risk, and the proximity formerly inherent in single combat, operated as deterrent factors to all but the most determined combatants. The use of a firearm, by contrast, is antiseptic and impersonal. It therefore presents a far more appealing option to the faint of heart, for the purposes of assault, homicide, or suicide. If for no other reason than this, the Way of the Western Warrior should include some experience with a classical weapons system.

Another unavoidable feature of modern society is the labyrinthine and burgeoning canon of civil and criminal law. Martial artists who venture into the outside world without any understanding of the legal implications of their status are at least negligent, not to mention highly vulnerable, and the teacher who fails to address this subject is either extremely reckless or willfully ignorant. Each country has developed a body of law with regard to the defense of self, others, and property, from the relatively liberal standards governing the use of force in certain American states to the somewhat more conservative European model. These are, in effect, the rules of engagement. How can a strategist hope to be victorious if he does not even understand the outermost contours of the applicable laws?

For example, many American states, but by no means all, impose on their citizenry a duty to retreat "to the wall," if it is safe to do so, before resorting to the use of lethal force in self-defense. In such so-called retreat jurisdictions, however, the duty generally does not apply if one is in his home, one is in his place of work, or one is the victim of certain violent crimes. The "defense of the home" exception to this general prohibition has in turn given rise to a common and potentially disastrous misperception that lethal force may be used, at least in certain jurisdictions, purely in the defense of property. For anyone whose armamentarium, martial or otherwise, includes potentially lethal weaponry, a rudimentary understanding of these principles is critical.

Knowing the rules, however, is not enough. In the heat of the moment, it would be unwise to commence a reasoned application of constitution, statute, and precedent to the present situation. The law must be distilled into various representative scenarios, and the legal, ethical, and tactical ramifications must be considered before the situation arises. What will you do if robbed by a masked attacker who holds the knife well back from you in a reverse grip? Some teachers advise you to throw your wallet in one direction and run in the other. Certain schools maintain that when the muzzle of a small arm is in contact with the body, it is theoretically possible to brush the weapon aside faster than the attacker can pull the trigger. Whatever one's tactical preference, the determination should be made well before the need to apply it ever arises.

On this subject, one more point must be made. At law, in the context of the use of force, there are rarely any clear and unambiguous rules. No magic combination of factors will automatically lead to acquittal or conviction. Each case is examined on an ad hoc basis. Therefore, one must keep one's faculties sharp and functional at all times. The aircraft cannot be left to fly on autopilot. At law, as in life, everything counts.

16. *KOJI* — THE MASTER TEXTS

History will be kind to me for I intend to write it.

—Sir Winston Churchill

From time to time, one comes across a virtuoso whose ability belies his years. Particularly in the related realms of mathematics, music, and chess, child prodigies are not uncommon. But in some contexts, however, such novelties are also logical impossibilities. The nonteaching sensei and the twenty-year-old master are good examples. The characters for sensei are strictly translated as "one who has gone before." If the sensei does not teach, he has no students. If there are no students, there is no dojo hierarchy. If there is no hierarchy, there is no one to have gone before. By virtue of pure logic then, the sensei must have students.

Similarly, to master a system is to know it deeply, to be able to apply all of its essential teachings and a number of variations besides, in a wide variety of contexts. Some refer to the quest for this ability as "finding the groove." To be a master-teacher is to know not only these principles but also the art of sharing them with others, and to understand it all so thoroughly that virtually no situation might arise which one cannot take firmly in hand. Some describe this as "responding before the echo of the question has faded away." The ability to do these things comes from experience. There is no shortcut. It cannot be replaced by shrewdness. Innate ability is no substitute and can, in fact, be a hindrance. It takes time.

By no means an alternative to direct engagement, the study of the master texts is, however, another essential component in the education of the warrior. Collected in the space of a few feet of bookshelf is the combined experience of ten-thousand years. Conditions one might prefer not to endure firsthand can be appreciated vicariously and appropriate lessons learned. One can live through both sides of the battle. One can learn from the way in which heroes have faced life and death.

There are certain universal principles, according to the master, the essential nature of which was understood by the ancients. These ideas resurface in various incarnations over time, perhaps with more detail or supporting evidence, but in a fashion that is fundamentally consistent with the wisdom of the past. For example, scientific trials continue to validate many of the theories underlying the practices of traditional Chinese medicine to such an extent that these modalities are gaining acceptance in certain Western medical spheres. By reading the ancient treatises, one has an opportunity to explore concepts that are likely to recur in modern science and philosophy, if not now, then soon.

One day the master was explaining the way in which a small expenditure of energy early on in a process could be equivalent to, or greater than, a much larger effort at a later point.[1] At length, one student began to understand. "Like chaos theory," he offered, drawing the analogy from a different field of his studies.

"Don't know this word," the master replied truthfully.

"You know, a butterfly flaps its wings in China, and a week later there's a storm in New York. You know, butterfly, moth," the student said, emphatically simulating beating wings with his hands and pointing at the nearby light fixture. The master considered this.

"Very good," he said at last. "Yes . . . like this. . . ." He mimicked the arm flapping, faintly. "*Kochou-jutsu*." The art of the butterfly.

Aside from the practical advantages of studying the ancient record, there is an even more compelling reason to read the master texts. Each new student of the martial tradition becomes a link in the chain extending out of the mists of antiquity and over the horizon of the future. While the conditions and priorities of society may change across time and space, the fundamental themes remain the same. By sharing the thoughts, words, and deeds of the ancient masters, we help preserve the continuity of the tradition—ryu, the flow.

1. According to the master, the nature of the process did not matter; fighting, fishing, or flower arranging to the strategist are all the same.

17. *NIHONGO*—THE LINGUA FRANCA

If you wish to learn the highest truths, begin with the alphabet.

—Japanese proverb

Every profession has its terms of art: *voir dire, mayday, stat, realpolitik, gestält.* Regardless of the nationality of the practitioner, the language of a classical vocation tends to retain vestiges of the culture from which it sprang or in which it flourished. The practice of medicine, at least until recently, required the student to absorb an astonishing quantity of Latin for gross anatomy purposes alone. The language of diplomacy, and therefore politics, has traditionally been French, perhaps as a result, at least in part, of its capacity for indirectness and nuance. As a consequence of the ascendancy of French culture during the Middle Ages, medieval English knights generally adopted a Gallic surname indicating their place of origin.

Falling somewhere between these two traditions in terms of its genesis, the *sine qua non* of the legal profession is that attorneys should mispronounce both Latin and French expressions with equal fluency. Thankfully, for the sake of travelers around the world, a consensus has been achieved with respect to the use of a single language in aviation—English. And it is perhaps instructive to note that the common language of the future may well consist entirely of ones and zeros.

In addition to reinforcing a commonality of cultural heritage, however, the adoption of a universal language in a particular field of endeavor serves more practical purposes as well. General acceptance of a *lingua franca* allows for clarity, uniformity, and precision of expression. The culture that is most responsible for the advent or flourishing of a discipline has typically spent a great deal of time thinking and writing about the subject and is therefore generally better equipped to provide analytical and descriptive tools of a linguistic nature. For example, the preferred language for the study of frozen precipitation might well be Inuit, with its multitude of expressions to describe the simple English word snow.

Japanese is an excellent candidate for an international language of the martial arts. The contributions to this field of study made by the people of that tiny island are profound and beyond question, and the volume of both its written and oral tradition is substantial. The language itself is both precise and simple. It contains many unique concepts and epigrammatic expressions that capture subtleties in ways often lost in translation. At the same time, the articulated structure of its phraseology allows for the expression of complex ideas through compound constructions with relative ease: for example, *ki-mono*, "wearing thing"; *kake-mono*, "hanging thing"; *maki-mono*, "rolled up thing."

Furthermore, the symbolism implicit in the ideographic evolution of the Chinese (and therefore Japanese) written language is particularly well suited to the task of capturing the figurative nature of many martial arts concepts. There are didactic opportunities in the grammatical structures of the language as well, with its hierarchy of honorific forms and its aversion to vulgar or gauche expressions. And the process of divining the meaning of compound ideographs from their component radicals is an instructive and educational process all by itself.

In characteristic defiance of convention, the master would issue promotion certificates some time *before* the date of a candidate's test. These diplomas cataloged the techniques in which proficiency would be required on the impending examination. It was an equally important part of the students' preparation that they translate their scroll in its entirety, delve into the ideographic components of each symbol, and be prepared to read, write, and respond to questions regarding the script of their art.

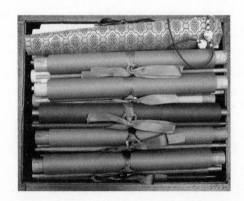

Whether one selects Japanese, Chinese, Tagalog, or some other language to describe one's art, efforts should be made to employ terminology precisely and correctly. Taking time to speak properly is a mark of respect not only to one's teachers but also to one's own self and one's students. And in accordance with the time-honored training principle, "show, don't say," a working knowledge of the vocabulary necessary to conduct a simple class can be achieved with relative ease.

18. *SHIKA, DOKA, RENGA—*
EXPRESSION

A fool sees not the same tree a wise man sees.

—William Blake

One day an apprentice asked the master why he encouraged the reading and writing of poetry among his students. Typically, the answer came in the form of a question. "When you first began training, why did you shout when performing certain techniques?"

"Because everyone else did," the student replied.

"And now why?" the master asked.

"Because it seems right. It is part of the inner feeling. It fits," the student said.

"Same thing," the master said.

Poetry and literature have long been associated with the

martial traditions of both the East and the West, for example, *The Tale of Genji*, *The Iliad*, and *Horatius at the Bridge*. At first blush, the coupling of the romantic muse and the martial spirit may seem an odd one. But hardly surprising is the stoic and ascetic demands of a warrior's lifestyle giving rise to expressive and creative urges while at the same time affording only rare and therefore special opportunities for their exercise.

Furthermore, the ability to compose verse on command, whether witty or profound, has historically been a valued commodity in the halls of court as a testament to the breadth of one's education as well as an example of grace under pressure. Poetry, therefore, may be seen as a kind of spiritual *corpus callosum* between the distinct hemispheres of the character of the gentleman-warrior. It allows at once for the expression and the conveyance of otherwise strictly controlled emotions. Like other pacific arts, its yin qualities also afford a delicate balance to the yang of the battlefield.

Most students of the Eastern tradition are familiar with the 5-7-5 structure of *haiku*, an epigrammatic form that seeks to capture the essence of a moment, season, or feeling. The most famous exponent of this mode of expression was Matsuo Basho, who abandoned his "banana house" to seek inspiration on the narrow road to a far province. Fewer people are familiar with *doka*, "poems of the Way." Past masters employed this form to convey some fundamental truth of training, and diligent attention to these bequests will often yield *oku*, "hidden teachings," to the discerning eye.

Renga, "linked verse," by contrast is generally a team sport. The first lyricist delivers a composition within the familiar 5-7-5 framework. The second participant must immediately produce a responsive 7-7 stanza. This practice, particularly in the form of the prearranged graduation tradition, can take on an almost theatrical quality.[2] Those who remain blind to the artistry of this form of expression are also deaf to the valuable lessons and venerable principles it contains. Their performance will always be lopsided, and their form will lack balance. According to the master, without yin, there can be no yang. The practice of poetry is both instructive and salutary, and a necessary part of advancement in the Way of the Western Warrior.

2. In the master's tradition, upon promoting a student to *shodan*, the teacher laments the burden of the solitary Way. With uncharacteristic defiance, the student issues a denial, maintaining that there are now two walking the same path together.

19. *HEIHO*—STRATEGY

Strategy is the craft of the warrior. Commanders must enact the craft and troopers should know this. There is no warrior in the world today who really understands the Way of strategy. There are various Ways. There is the Way of salvation by the law of Buddha, the Way of Confucius governing the Way of learning, the Way of healing as a doctor, as a poet teaching the Way of waka, tea, archery, and many arts and skills. Each man practices as he feels inclined.

—Miyamoto Musashi

The dojo's outer door had a tendency to shut loudly with a bang when there was the slightest breeze. The master would always reach his hand backward upon entering, to prevent this from happening. The significance of this attention to detail became apparent one day when he told the story of the three sons and the pail of water. Eager to impress a visiting dignitary with his family's martial prowess, a father balanced a bucket of water on the lintel atop the door and called for his youngest son. Upon entering, the boy responded to the falling object by drawing his blade and striking it aside in one motion while spraying water across the *shoji* but remaining relatively dry himself. The experiment was repeated for the second son, who also sprung the trap, but managed to catch the bucket before it spilled, and then placed it back atop the door. The eldest son, when summoned in a similar fashion, had the foresight to glance upward before opening the door fully, and seeing the bucket, simply removed it before entering.

One of the master's more advanced lessons in Kishido involved trying to lead an opponent to engage in a certain behavior through indirect encouragement alone. Just as in curling where the competitor polishes his stone's preferred path with a brush, so the student is asked, for example, to arrange a room so that the next person to enter will naturally select a particular seat, ostensibly of his own free will. Consistent with the principle of the winding way, this practice is built upon the theory that an indirect attack is more difficult to evade. It is a matter of heiho.

There are many ways to study strategy. In the *Go Rin No Sho*, Musashi intimates that the study of the sword is, in truth, the study of strategy. In light of the measured pace required for a proper stroke with the long sword, particularly when wielded in katate, the *kenjutsu-ka* must appreciate the wisdom of this assertion. To strike without calculating one's next move is likely to leave the swordsman with no fallback position, should his initial attack fail to find its mark.

Sadly, all too often the importance of strategy is ignored on the modern battlefield to disastrous effect. Some might argue that the study of strategy is less critical in an age of such technological sophistication. Computers, satellites, and machinery determine the mobilization, deployment, and engagement of forces. Modern armed forces have no need of a strategist, they say. They are wrong. Their position is simplistic, and the depth of their analysis rarely rises above the tactical level. It is always advisable to "box clever," even when equipped with superior firepower. It is also more elegant. Whenever asked to comment on a student's performance of a particular technique, the master would invariably respond with one of two suggestions: "Very powerful, more beauty" or "Very beautiful, more power."

The way of strategy lives on in the experienced commander's campaigns, the litigation attorney's courtroom, and the capital city's corridors of political power. It is also manifest in humankind's abiding fascination with the game of chess, pitting assets against one another in a series of individual engagements, and its Eastern counterpart, *go*, in which stones are deployed in a parallel fashion to capture territory and choke off the opponent's lines of supply. The gentleman-warrior should study such ways.

20. *KOAN*—MUMONKAN

In the pursuit of learning, every day something is acquired. In the pursuit of Tao, less and less is done until non-action is achieved. When nothing is done, nothing is left undone. The world is ruled by letting things take their course. It cannot be ruled by interfering.

—*Tao Te Ching*

Whenever the master shared a *koan* with a student, he would take down a weathered box from the *tokonoma* and extract some small item—a pin, a scrap of paper, a ring—to accompany the assignment. The gift was not supposed to suggest an answer, for according to the master there were no answers in the discipline of koan. Rather, it was symbolic of a possible response, for in each mundane article, the master had, in his time, discovered some truth.

We live today in an age of instant gratification. Nourishment, information, and entertainment are rarely more than the push of a button away. As recently as the last generation, for example, undertaking any serious research assignment generally required poring over dusty tomes in the chilly, third-floor reading room of some inconveniently located library, but with the advent of the Internet, even the need for this type of quest is facing extinction. The only solution, therefore, is to raise one's expectations.

Some knowledge does not come easily. Penetrating the mysteries of a particular kata, for example, can take years of study, turning the matter over in one's hand, wearing it smooth from use, and memorizing its every ridge and wrinkle, in the process. So it is with koan. As with haiku, koan seeks to express the inexpressible. The capacity for lateral thinking is perhaps a symptom rather than a goal of koan, for the only way to convey such subtle ideas is by analogy. Imagine, for example, trying to describe the color red to another who has never seen it. One can allude to the flavor of warmth or flame,

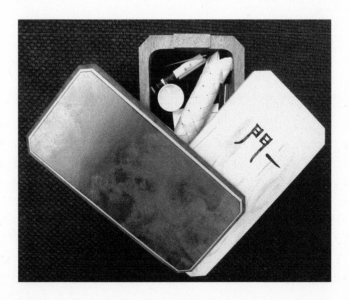

but until the other looks on it for himself, descriptions are no better than stick drawings in the sand.

The substance of the koan in *Mumonkan*, in particular, expresses sentiments of value to the warrior. The absence of a thing, the true nature of an item and *satori*, the prick of a pin—these are all concepts that will stand the traveler in good stead along the way. It is difficult to say more on the subject. Take down the box for yourself. Select an icon. Meditate on its meaning. Be patient. The truth will reveal itself.

21. *KANPO*—HEALING

The life so short, the craft so long to learn.

—Hippocrates

After an exhausting class, the master indulged in a game. This was quite unusual. "Do as I do," he instructed. He picked up his glass. His partner did likewise. He placed it on top of his head. So did the student. He held it at arm's length. His actions were mirrored. He drank the contents. So did his reflection. He placed his glass on the table in front of him. The other joined it. He picked it up again, placed it to his mouth, and refilled it with the *sake* that he had evidently not swallowed. His partner, of course, could not follow suit. "Take care not to do a thing you cannot also undo," he said, his meaning clear. Then he laughed.

There is an established tradition that senior practitioners

of the martial arts should also know the rudiments of healing. The attainment of this objective is facilitated by the consonance of the theories underlying these overtly antithetical pursuits. At its highest level, the study of *kyusho-jutsu* is virtually indistinguishable from *shin-jutsu*. The sensitivity of touch required to execute *kuzushi*, in the course of a throw, can also be used to heal, in the practice of *reiki*. The anatomical discoveries made by Minamoto Yoshimitsu's dissection of corpses, which contributed to the foundation of the Daito Ryu style of *aikijujutsu*, are no different in substance from Galen's anatomical studies in the ancient Greek city of Pergamum during the second century. They are different faces of the same coin.

Knowledge of healing can take many forms. For example, during a childhood riding lesson, a particularly large and headstrong horse crushed the master's foot. So bad was the injury that doctors feared the master might never walk again and could offer little in the way of therapy. Luckily, a family elder had experience with certain traditional forms of natural healing. In defiance of the conventional prognosis, the injured foot was treated with a series of herbal poultices. Within a few days, the swollen, purple stump mutated back into something resembling a foot, albeit a tender one, yellowed by maturing bruises. Within a week, the master was walking after a fashion. Within a month, there was no remnant of the injury at all, other than a lesson in the value of alternative paths to a common goal.

Rather than merely seeking to mask the symptoms of pathology by dulling the senses with chemicals, Oriental medicine looks to the environment for causes and to the natural world for solutions. The therapeutic and analgesic properties of many ancient remedies are only now achieving recognition in the Western medical community. The recency of this phenomenon is particularly ironic in that Hippocrates, the acknowledged father of Western medicine, contemplated considerations such as the weather, the quality of drinking water, and the paths of favorable winds in his treatise *Airs, Waters, and Places*, two and a half millennia ago.

It is said in the martial arts that the sword that takes life can also give life. Quite apart from the cosmological balance achieved by embracing this bifurcated approach to martial training, a very practical consideration also arises—the master of a dojo may well be called upon to administer triage to an injured student at some point until help arrives. For this reason, the rudiments of first aid should be considered integral to the education of a martial arts teacher. Laws have been passed in many jurisdictions, in fact, requiring that a CPR-certified first responder be on hand whenever and wherever strenuous physical activity takes place in an institutional setting.

To delay preparation until a situation is emergent is the hallmark of the foolhardy. The superior warrior employs his superior skills to avoid a situation in which he will be forced to call upon them.

22. *KOMUSO*—THE MASTER'S FLUTE

If attacked from the light, I will strike back in the light.
If attacked from the dark, I will strike back in the dark.
If attacked from all directions, I will strike back like a
  whirlwind.
If attacked from emptiness, I will lash out like a flail.

—*Fuke Zenji*

As the stories of the master make clear, he was a man possessed of many talents. In the course of his travels, he also accumulated many things of inestimable worth—more a product of their rarity than any intrinsic value. The array of intricately carved drawers in his desk housed yellowing scrolls of techniques handed down from master to student for generations, keepsakes received from friends and colleagues occupying a wide variety of stations, and mementos from countless adventures in faraway lands.

Among these was a flute. But it was no ordinary flute. It was a *shakuhachi*, whose name is a corruption of the term *I shaku hachi sun*, referring to the length of the instrument. This particular shakuhachi was very old and rare. It had been crafted from heavy bamboo—hard enough to strike heads, both light and dark, if necessary—and boasted an ebony *utaguchi*, "blowing edge." It had been in his family for generations. As a result of both its size and its worth, the shakuhachi enjoyed a place of pride on a purpose-built shelf above the master's desk.

The truly remarkable thing about the master was not so much that he possessed such rare treasures—both corporeal and cerebral—but that he was so willing to share them, free of charge, with any worthy applicant. Where some might have been concerned that others would appropriate their ideas or methods to advantage, without remuneration, the master was not. "This is to be shared," he would say. Where others might have worried that a borrower would damage their irreplaceable artifacts, the master did not. "These are for using," he would simply say as he entrusted prized possessions to some new student. In this way, he was not so much concerned with the getting and the having as with the giving and the sharing.

When asked about this extraordinary generosity, the master explained it this way: As a child, his family had experienced a period of great deprivation during the war. One day, his mother had come home from her job with a gift for him—a highly unusual occurrence in many ways. It was a small box of writing paper. So valuable was this commodity that the master immediately wrapped it up and tucked it under his bed for safekeeping. Once in a while he would take the box out and look at the clean white sheets within, but he never dared to write on them. Years later, when the family's fortunes had improved considerably, the master happened across this hidden treasure again. He recognized at that moment that this thing of extraordinary past value had virtually no present worth, and it saddened him that he had not made use of it at a time when it would have meant so much.

At that moment, the master recognized that things were for using. In fact, he came to prefer items that improved with use—a well broken in pair of boots, a favorite jacket, or a musical instrument that grew into itself and its user. The corollary to this theory was that if an object could not withstand repeated use, it probably was not worth having in the first place. The master's shakuhachi, for example, had been passed down from teacher to student many times and lovingly maintained, repaired, and restored over the years. As a result, it learned to produce a rich and resonant tone that newer models simply could not match. The shakuhachi, like its master, improved with use and age. It is perhaps for this reason that there are no child prodigies in the discipline of the shakuhachi. None.

One day a young student of the master's expressed an interest in playing the shakuhachi—his ancient and valuable shakuhachi. The master took it down from its shelf without hesitation and handed it over to the young one. His more senior students cringed at the boldness of the request, thinking it akin to a novice asking to handle a master swordsman's blade, but the master seemed oblivious to the perceived *faux pas*. He was happy to share. According to his school of thought, flutes are for playing; paper is for writing; life is for living.

23. *CHUSHIN*—BALANCE

A human being should be able to change a diaper,
plan an invasion, butcher a hog, conn a ship, design a
building, write a sonnet, balance accounts, build a
wall, set a bone, comfort the dying, take orders, give
orders, cooperate, act alone, solve equations, analyze
a new problem, pitch manure, program a computer,
cook a tasty meal, fight efficiently, die gallantly.
Specialization is for insects.

—Robert Heinlein

There was a birth in the dojo. Not the master's child, but
one could have been mistaken for thinking so in light of the
attention he devoted to this tiny addition to the martial family. Gone was the stern countenance and gruff voice, and in
its place was the beaming, cooing expression of a doting
grandparent. A celebration was planned, and the interruption

of other matters by occasional cries from beyond the mat was greeted with a laugh rather than a frown. This surprised many of the students who had, until this point, only known the man as a master of the martial arts and had perhaps failed to appreciate the depth and breadth of that term as it applied to this particular individual.

As children take their first, few, faltering steps in this world, one witnesses too often more established residents trampling past—and sometimes over—these newcomers, both driven and blinded by their own wants and needs. And as anyone familiar with the art of bonsai can attest, tiny branches are easily bent and broken. In the master's tradition, therefore, great pains were taken to avoid what he described as "crushing the spirit." When in the company of children, his voice was soft and his attitude permissive to a degree that those who had endured some of his more challenging examinations found shocking. "Any wild horse can be tamed in time," he said, "but if the animal lacks spirit, what would be the point?"

Further discussion and research revealed that this liberal approach dominated until the age of five—a seminal birthday in the tradition of the ancient warrior houses. That auspicious anniversary signaled a transition from the total protection provided by the cloak of infancy to the first glimmerings illuminating the path that the warrior-child would one day walk. The corresponding ceremony—known in the West as *adoptio per arma*—was among the most important for parent and child alike.

On the eve of the birthday, the young warrior was to be bathed, to be dressed in white, and to have his hair and nails trimmed in anticipation of the following day's event. But far more important than these physical preparations was the internal aspect of the process. Throughout the child's life, but most especially on the night before his ceremony, his parents

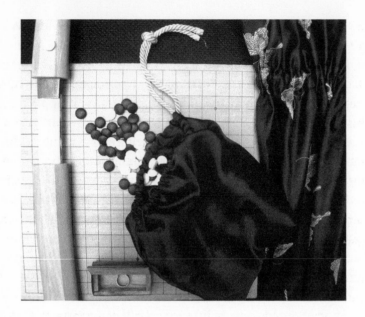

were charged with ensuring that they had begun to instill the rudiments of the values and ideals that would be the warrior's lifelong companions in his journey along the way. It would likely fall to some other person, at some other time, to teach the young one *how* to fight, but it was never too early to begin the discussion of *when* to fight and, perhaps of even greater importance, when not to.

During the ceremony itself, the child would be presented by an existing member of the tradition and made to stand on a go board. His toy wooden sword would then be replaced with a real one. Other details varied from family to family. Some required the selection of a stone from an opaque bag, its color being thought to prophesy the path the young warrior would someday walk. Others involved a short question-and-answer session with the candidate, to ensure that the parents had done their job properly. Whatever the variations, the result was the same. The child had embarked on a life-long journey.

In the midst of all this excitement, the new father was somewhat downcast. It was not just the lack of sleep and the fraying of the nerves attendant to all such new arrivals; it was also a sense of loss. His studies—both martial and academic—had begun to suffer noticeably as a result of this new and pressing demand on his time and resources, and he was not coping all that well. The more he struggled to force thirty hours of activity into a twenty-four-hour day, the less well equipped he was to deal with the time he did have. On those occasions when he could still get to the dojo, he tended to stay long after class had ended, almost reluctant to return to his new life.

On one such evening, the master returned silently to the darkened training hall and watched his young charge trying to internalize a new form over and over again, determination and frustration vying for the upper hand. When the student was finished, the master approached. He placed a knowing hand on the young father's shoulder. "There are three things you must do to be a man: Have a child. Plant a tree. Write a book. You are almost halfway there." So saying, he handed over a small package wrapped in brown paper and then melted back into the shadows again. Inside was a beautiful leather-bound book filled with blank pages—and an acorn. In time the student came to realize that the most important book is the one you have yet to write, and that the most important part of life is what you leave behind.

24. *GARYOTENSEI*—THE EYES OF THE DRAGON

God is in the details.

—Ludwig Mies Van Der Rohe

"**Plant your rear heel firmly.** Enter more deeply. Keep your eyes on your opponent. Don't forget the retraction. Again! Relax! Remember to breathe!" Some teachers tend to overwhelm students with a detailed list of requirements for a given technique and then criticize their inevitable failure to perform one or other aspect of the waza perfectly the first time. They do this with all the subtlety of a band saw. The master's approach was exactly the opposite. He would begin by demonstrating only the grossest of motor movements required to lumber through a technique, likening this first step to hacking off a suitable branch. Thus, the initial phase was relatively easy to achieve and remember. Then began the process of refinement. Each iteration thereafter would generate some new suggestion or correction, shaping the raw material in gradual stages, working the wood toward its eventual form. Some students found this method frustrating. When asked how long it would take to get it right, the master invariably replied, "A lifetime."

In the art of woodworking, it is true that the desired shape can often be achieved quickly through the vigorous application of powerful tools. The wood can, in effect, be beaten into submission. With the right equipment, one can cut across the grain and cleanly through the knothole. But the finished product lacks any hint of the natural beauty of its previous incarnation. Trees are living things, and while they can be coaxed and cajoled into following one course or another, they have a will of their own. By working patiently with the grain, wood can be persuaded to adopt a particular shape, without sacrificing the individuality of the particular piece, producing a cooperative result that reflects both the nature of the material and the hand of the artisan.

A measure of proficiency in the rudiments of self-defense can be achieved in relatively short order. Most military and law-enforcement courses in unarmed combat convey a substantial degree of skill in a matter of weeks or months. The study of a martial art, however, is a discipline of a lifetime. If the goal is mere domination in the sphere of single combat, then the student should seek out the most expedient route to this destination. Kishido is not this way. Like the *kyudo-ka*, the goal of the practitioner of Kishido is to refine the spirit. Striking the heart of the *mato* is merely an inconsequential side effect. For every aim achieved, another target appears. In every endeavor, infinite detail is to be captured, or as Japanese idiom renders it, the student must continually strive to "paint the eyes on the dragon." The process is endless.

PART THREE

Strategy

25. *KETSUBUN* — THE MISSING MASS

I think a true master, and one who is not so only in name, should have a good heart. . . . He should have a positive effect on all those with whom he comes into contact.

—Onuma Hideharu

One night while traveling home from the dojo on the train, a student was attacked and beaten quite badly by a gang of local toughs. It was no accident that the last train of the night ran shortly after closing time at the pubs, and especially on the weekends, it was not unusual for a very merry crowd of revelers to pile into the carriages for this last ride home. It was also not unusual for there to be a few rude exchanges between "town and gown," given that many of the indigenous young men and women were resentful of the ivory-towered immigrants who populated their town's campus for nine months of the year. But it was unusual, and in fact unprecedented, for violence of this magnitude to occur.

No one was quite sure how it had happened. The assailants were unknown and the victim was not talking. His injuries were mostly superficial—lumps and bumps—but he had withdrawn into his shell after the incident, missing classes at both the college and the dojo for several days. The former went unnoticed by the instructors, but not the latter. When the master asked after the student, his friends murmured something to the effect that he was ill, for fear of upsetting the master on a number of grounds. They maintained this fiction for as long as they could until it became clear to all that the boy would not be returning. It was then that the master made his first house call.

Not the very next day, but the day after that, the injured boy was back on the mat, gingerly making his way through rolls and falls. Over the months that followed, the other students were able to piece together at least some of what had transpired. The boy was small and slight, but very skilled. Perhaps for both reasons, when approached by the group of drunken thugs on the train, he ignored everything the master had taught him, and if he had not exactly started the fight, he certainly did not try to defuse the situation either. The hard lesson he had learned is that all other things being equal, the bigger yang usually wins. But that was not the true revelation.

The master's unexpected visit to his dorm room and the conversation that ensued behind those closed doors precipitated a period of deep contemplation and reflection by the student on the true nature and purpose of the martial arts.

From this meditation, the student emerged with a wisdom beyond his years—a wisdom that is sadly lacking among too many members of the modern martial community.

What the young warrior had realized then was this: With the exception of a very few, specialized professions, unarmed combat is no longer a societal imperative. The time when a man might be called upon to defend himself, his family, or his honor with physical force is largely a thing of the past. This was not to say that the occasional fight would not occur as the student learned first hand. But he knew that this was the exception, not the rule. He knew that it could have been averted. And he also knew that all his martial training had failed to carry the day.

Those who wish to defend themselves against threats have been able to do so easily and quickly for centuries, by simply paying a visit to the local gunsmith. Even in the realm of purely unarmed combat, a few, effective combat techniques can be learned in the space of a couple of weeks at a self-defense class. Those who want to improve their fitness can do so very efficiently and comfortably with the help of the machinery available at almost any local gymnasium. Neither of these goals requires the kind of dedication and commitment that comes with the proper study of any true martial art.

Those who choose to follow the way of the warrior—to walk the path of the master—quickly come to realize that its demands are extreme but its rewards sublime, transcending such trivia as one's resting pulse rate or win-loss record. It is the voyage of a lifetime. Accordingly, the journey and not the destination is what matters, and for those who can appreciate this truth, there is beauty at each turn and new discovery around every corner.

26. *YOHEI*—MERCENARIES AND MERCHANTS

If we look at the world we see arts for sale. Men use equipment to sell themselves. As if with the nut and the flower, the nut has become less than the flower. In this kind of Way of strategy, both those teaching and those learning the way are concerned with coloring and showing off their technique, trying to hasten the bloom of the flower. They speak of "this dojo" and "that dojo." They are looking for profit.

—Miyamoto Musashi

The master was greatly enamored of what he called the protective power of poverty. He delighted in telling the story of the itinerant monk with nothing more to his name than a wooden bowl that he used for begging. It seems that while making his way along a high cliff one day, the bowl fell from his grasp and was smashed into countless pieces on the rock face below. "Free at last!" the monk said. The master would then laugh heartily.

When the master was still a young man, a great fighter from the United States came to visit his country. It was said that the foreigner knew something of kochou-jutsu—the art of the butterfly, but could also sting like a bee. Since the master's name was well known in his province, members of the American's entourage approached him and asked if he would agree to engage in an exhibition bout with their man. The master was, of course, willing to extend any courtesy in his power to welcome another warrior in the spirit of comradeship, and they began to discuss the arrangements. Then, the matter of money came up. How much would the master expect to be paid? The master merely shook his head. It was not proper to discuss such matters. Next, the question of his amateur status was raised. According to the American's contract, he could only fight with professional boxers, so the master would have to agree to be recognized in some capacity by the sport's governing body. This was too much. The master simply walked away.

Matters of finance have always been considered vulgar in the martial tradition. In the East, warriors who shopped their services to the highest bidder were considered *eta*. In ancient Japan, necessary payments were often wrapped in abalone, a far more acceptable medium for the purposes of exchange. To this day, in fact, envelopes with pictures or characters symbolizing the ancient custom are still employed for this purpose in polite society. Similarly, the Beefeaters, yeoman guards of the British monarchy, take their name from the fact that they were originally compensated for their services in trade, as the term suggests.

In order that his art's purity not be debased by mercantilism or hampered by financial considerations, the master adopted a very simple rule: No charging. Full stop. No tuition. No contribution. No membership dues. No testing fee. Never. No money changed hands. This is not to say, however, that no one pays. The cost is just measured in a currency that does not feature on the exchange markets. It is not subject to inflation or devaluation. It cannot be wired between accounts. It is a constant. It is measured in dedication, loyalty, and obligation. Kishido is not for everyone. Its lessons are difficult, and its practice demanding.

The master's approach should in no way be seen to impugn the commendable skill with which some teachers are able to navigate the treacherous waters between the Scylla of insolvency and the Charybdis of corruption, remaining true to their art. One's true motivation in pursuing the way is largely a personal matter. It should be noted, however, that those who enjoy teaching for a living generally do so in spite of the financial aspects and not because of them. Those for whom the martial arts are nothing more than a financial opportunity can never be considered practitioners of the way.

One way to honor this principle, the master suggested, was to maintain interests and activities outside the martial realm. While one might envy full-time martial arts teachers, who can dedicate every waking minute to their art and dojo, for the practitioner of Kishido, the associated risk is simply too great. Such a teacher is dependent on students for survival, with all the attendant conflicts of interest this may invite. Such an arrangement also lacks the equilibrium and the challenge of having to attend to multiple callings. Such an approach tends to make oneself the focus of one's studies. This is not to deny the possibility that teachers may be paid for their services and yet remain true to their principles. This was simply not the master's way. In his dojo, and more importantly, in his heart, the master fixed the following words:

> *To set the cause above renown,*
> *To love the game beyond the prize,*
> *To honor, while you strike him down,*
> *The foe that comes with fearless eyes;*
> *To count the life of battle good,*
> *And dear the land that gave you birth,*
> *And dearer yet the brotherhood*
> *That binds the brave of all the earth.*
>
> —Sir Henry Newbolt

27. *GI*—RIGHT DECISION

Think of the going out before you enter.

—Arabian proverb

Most traditional schools of *kyudo*, "traditional Japanese archery," focus on some variation of the *hassetsu shaho*—the eight positions of the archer. These postures are generally regarded as still shots or representative stages in the fluid kata of shooting an arrow. While most of these schools also teach some of the formalities that traditionally precede and follow the exercise of shooting, the master's lessons focused on these ostensibly ancillary aspects of the art perhaps more than the taking of the shot itself.

To begin with, students were taught *uchine-jutsu* (the all but forgotten art of using the unstrung bow as a kind of flexible staff) and *yajiri* (arrowheads) and even *ya* (arrows) as projectile weapons. The idea was that the archer should know how to defend himself should he encounter an attacker prior to *nyujo* (approaching the firing point and preparing his weapon to shoot). Adherence to such ancient practices is one of the primary factors that distinguishes *kyujutsu* from kyudo.

Of perhaps even more important are the processes of *sadamenoza* and *honza* (decision sitting and book sitting). In sadamenoza, having prepared the bow to fire, the archer takes a moment to consider his natural environment. In addition to selecting the optimal firing point, determining the effect of the position of the sun and other natural phenomena, and establishing the preferred sequence of shots, an appropriate strategy must be selected from the wide variety of available possibilities. As in kenjutsu, this is a matter of heiho. It is to be performed from a position of relative safety prior to engaging the enemy. More tactical matters, such as target acquisition, the appropriate type of yajiri for each particular target, and compensating for windage and elevation are accomplished during honza.

Beyond this type of practice, the master also required that his students read and reflect upon the master texts. Perhaps required is too strong a word. Encouraged. The master would frequently allude to a particular treatise or term of art, almost in passing, and sometimes as a kind of intercultural shorthand. Unless the student has some familiarity with the subject matter, the reference would be meaningless, the insight lost.

In the arts, as in life, sufficient observation and reflection will generally yield an appropriate answer to virtually any problem. So to recognize the importance of doing one's homework is vital before rushing headlong into a situation and to believe firmly that a solution exists. Having discovered the correct course of action, however, following that path to its final destination is an entirely different matter.

28. *YU* — BRAVERY

Courage is not the absence of fear, but rather the
judgment that something else is more important
than fear.

—Ambrose Redmoon

A student once had to make an oral defense of his thesis at
the university. When preparing for this trial, he often found
himself short of breath, anxiety rising up in his chest like a
thickening fog and threatening to choke off his words. He
sought the master's counsel. The master reminded the student of the exercise in which the *obi* is cinched tightly around
the upper chest, and asked, "Why do we do this?"

"To learn to breathe from the abdomen," the student
replied.

"Why is this important?" the master asked. "Could you not
breathe before learning this?"

"Well, yes," the student responded, "but by breathing from the belly, we avoid becoming winded in the heat of shiai."

"Try breathing this way," the master advised.

At the moment of crisis, the body has a natural tendency to betray us. Heartbeat accelerates; respiration becomes more rapid; muscles tense; perspiration increases; blood vessels constrict; spontaneous shivering occurs; pupils dilate; saliva flow decreases; and epinephrine surges. Paradoxically, this so-called fight or flight response can reduce one's combat efficiency significantly. Fine motor movements are hampered by shaking, tension, and sweat. Air is in short supply. Dehydration can occur. The goal, therefore, is to control this response.

The first step is the practice of controlled abdominal breathing that can have a positive psychological and physiological effect on panic. It is one of the few autonomic functions capable of conscious control, and this line of communication between ego and id can be exploited to powerful effect. The true theater of engagement, however, is not in the thoracic cavity, but in the mind. While the elimination of fear completely may never be possible or even desirable, certain steps can be taken to manage it. As threshold matter, it is easier to remain confident, secure in the knowledge that the cause is just. In addition to ensuring that one is on the right side of a conflict, one must assure oneself that all possible alternatives to confrontation have been considered.

Knowing that a clash is inevitable, the next step is to have confidence in one's training. Anyone who studies the martial arts with regularity is likely to be well equipped relative to the typical adversary, and one can only hope that any truly serious student of the martial arts has matured beyond the point of picking fights. Furthermore, it is rare in modern society that one is faced with life-threatening combat.[1] Thus, while there is always a better fighter around the corner, you must proceed with self-assurance. One who dwells on the possibility of losing has already lost.

Finally, it is often helpful to consider the alternative. When beset by the voices of pessimism, take a moment to consider whether withdrawal is really a legitimate option. If it is, it should be considered. But more often than not, a direct confrontation of the alternative will reveal it for what it is—the whimpering of a child afraid of the dark. Take a deep breath, and step forward to face the music. This was the master's teaching.

---

1. This is to be distinguished from the very real possibility of being the victim of a violent crime, a matter discussed in more detail elsewhere in this text.

29. *JIN* — BENEVOLENCE

Look to be treated by others as you have treated others.

—Publilius Syrus

The master was generally willing to answer any question properly put to him, but was frequently reserved or evasive when asked about particular details of more dangerous techniques, especially when posed by newer students. He was understandably concerned that such skills should never be used for improper purposes. How he decided to whom he could entrust such teachings was something of a mystery. It was certainly not based solely on time served, since admission to the rarefied atmosphere of advanced classes occurred at different times for different students of the same cohort.

In a traditional dojo, there is a profound emphasis on respect—for the tradition, for the master, and for the other students. As is to be expected, the seniors ensured that juniors understood this principle so that the master himself never had to endure the embarrassment of having to administer discipline for inappropriate behavior. On occasion, however, he would have an opportunity to observe his students interacting with outsiders—on the way to and from the dojo, at the occasional public function, and during open mat sessions when he would busy himself with some menial task, perhaps attending to his bonsai, but always keeping a watchful eye on the practice. He seemed especially attentive to instances in which his deshi were dealing with their equals or subordinates—prospective students, novices, groundskeepers, and janitors. Those who accorded a similar level of respect to all people, regardless of rank, coincidently seemed to receive like treatment from the master.

Dealing with clumsy or inept students presents an age-old dilemma for the martial arts teacher. On one hand, one must maintain the highest possible standards in the art; on the other, who can benefit from the teachings of a martial way more than the naturally challenged? There are obviously disabilities that absolutely preclude certain goals, such as the loss of a sense or limb that can render some techniques impossible to perform. But apart from these extreme situations, almost anything can be achieved with sufficient patience. And in this capacity the teacher who was himself a naturally gifted student may encounter more difficulty than the one who struggled to achieve a measure of proficiency.

Throughout this process, one must remember that the effect of even the most powerful weapon depends entirely on the direction in which it is aimed. In Kishido, the most superb technique, the strongest fighter, the most impressive dojo, all are worth less than nothing if they pursue malevolent ends.

Some people speak of the dark arts, particularly when discussing some of the more lethal weapons and techniques in the martial armamentarium, but this is nonsense. There are no dark arts, only dark pursuits. Remember that enlightened warriors use their skills for benevolent purposes. Be deferential. Be gentle. Be kind.

30. *REI* — RIGHT ACTION

The United States Attorney is the representative not of an ordinary party to a controversy, but of a sovereignty whose obligation to govern impartially is as compelling as its obligation to govern at all; and whose interest, therefore, in a criminal prosecution is not that it shall win a case, but that justice shall be done. As such, he is in a peculiar and very definite sense the servant of the law, the twofold aim of which is that guilt shall not escape or innocence suffer. He may prosecute with earnestness and vigor—indeed, he should do so. But, while he may strike hard blows, he is not at liberty to strike foul ones. It is as much his duty to refrain from improper methods calculated to produce a wrongful conviction as it is to use every legitimate means to bring about a just one.

—*Berger v. U.S.*, 295 U.S. 78 (1935)

To do the right thing is not always easy, and fear is not always what urges a more cautious course of action. Fear is an obvious opponent. He is easy to recognize. Self-interest, so

115

often cloaked in justification, is harder to spot. The line of semantic demarcation between expedience and profitability may be a fine one, but it is there if you look for it. And one must recognize the true nature of the motivation underlying one's own acts and the acts of others and accept the associated costs.

This is not to suggest that unbridled altruism is to be embraced ubiquitously. There is a time for prioritizing one's own needs, for allowing oneself to falter because of inattentiveness to selfish necessities does no one any good. Once having realized that a thing should be done, the true follower of the Western warrior's way is charged with its performance, however little appeal the endeavor may hold. It is a matter of principle.

Pursuing the appropriate course will sometimes even require putting oneself in harm's way. It is not always enough merely to respond to the circumstances with which one is confronted; on occasion, it becomes necessary to seek out confrontation. Many times, this simply requires the asking of questions. One may encounter a situation that appears satisfactory on its surface, but at the same time sense that there is more to it than meets the eye. Whatever the vestigial faculty that provides this warning, and however tempting it may be to rely on the mere appearance of propriety, there exists a duty to make further inquiry, to seek the truth, to see justice done.

As is so often the case, conversations with the master's wife provided a great deal of insight into the man. While she was at least as circumspect as her husband was in terms of what she chose to reveal about their personal life, there was an undercurrent of pride that permitted the occasional modest disclosure. She would mention in passing that he had stayed at the dojo late into the night working with a particular student, or he had spent the bulk of the weekend reviewing written examinations. Whether he would have preferred to be doing something else was not known. It was certain, however, that when duty called, his answer was always yes. It was simply his way.

31. *MAKOTO*—TRUTH

Sir Thomas More: When a man takes an oath he is holding his own self in his hands, like water. If he opens his fingers then, he needn't hope to find himself again.

—Robert Bolt, *A Man for All Seasons*

When the master first came to the West, he and his wife were subjected to proper introductions on the university's venerated cocktail circuit. Some time later, the master confessed to having been perplexed by the conduct of the members of this select society. "We should have dinner sometime; you must come up to visit us; we'll certainly stop by when we're in the neighborhood." The sentiments expressed in these platitudes, it seemed to him, were false. When he was been invited to visit someone's home, an *on*, had been assumed. Suitable gifts would have to be procured; an auspicious and mutually agreeable date selected. The host's subsequent failure to follow through on this invitation was unthinkable. This bothered the master for a time, until he came to understand that such banal chatter amounted to no more than pleasant background noise in this context.

While the insincerity of superficial pleasantries common to many societal functions may only cause mild distress to some, the matter of one's word is a far more serious business altogether. The taking of an oath is reserved for the weightiest of undertakings: the covenant of marriage, the assumption of public office, the giving of testimony. Despite the ease with which fabrications seem to trip from so many tongues, swearing to the truth of a matter still seems to carry with it a certain authority even in modern society. As well it should. With the proliferation of contracts, waivers, and methods of electronic transaction, it seems there is little room left for dealing on a simple handshake. The days when one's word was his bond are of largely historical interest. Yet there are still a few endeavors in which trustworthiness should remain of paramount importance: public service, national security, education, and the realms of medical, legal, and financial confidentiality. Sadly, these are the very spheres that honesty is currently feeling the weather most acutely.

Whether or not one believes that violation of an oath will invite retribution, earthly or otherwise, is largely irrelevant in the Way of the Western Warrior. The greatest and most insidious deception is that of self. To abide by a rule for fear of punishment is no great achievement. To follow the path of truth for the sake of one's own integrity—that is an accomplishment and a challenge each time it is undertaken.

32. *MEIYO*—A MATTER OF HONOR

The reputation of a thousand years may be determined by the conduct of one hour.

—Japanese proverb

In the grips of examination fever, the students quizzed each other relentlessly. Their knowledge of history and custom as well as relevant terminology, language, and calligraphy would be probed extensively. In addition to drilling kata to the point of reflex, they tested their waza by surprising one another with a variety of attacks at unguarded moments.[2] There were also various skill-specific tasks to be mastered. The ability to extinguish a candle with a single strike without touching flame or wax was one such task.

On test day, they all arrived fully equipped to demonstrate this and other newfound abilities. They were therefore somewhat surprised and disappointed when the master merely

2. This latter practice was, in retrospect, perhaps somewhat reckless, but entirely consistent with the ardor of youth.

asked whether they had achieved these goals and accepted their responses without further inquiry. Didn't he want proof? How could he know that they had in fact done as they said? When asked about his reaction at a later date, the master seemed genuinely puzzled. Of course he had accepted their word on the matter. It was simply a matter of honor.

One's honor is worth exactly as much as its owner decides it is. For some, it is an inconvenient, unwieldy notion. Since it serves no concrete purpose, they give it little thought. For the practitioner of Kishido, it is one of the few possessions of any consequence. Like one's word, its present measure is defined by past performance. For those descended from an honorable line, it is a sacred inheritance to be safeguarded at all costs. For every one, it will be a legacy—either good or bad. It is merely borrowed for a season.

Few people can reflect on their lifetime's conduct to date without some cause for shame. Most travelers along the way have stumbled many times. To abandon noble aspirations because of past mistakes is to concede defeat. The path is not easy, and the high way is not for the faint of heart. In the master's tradition, the morning dew is believed to be sent to wash away the residue of the previous day's events. It prevents drowning in one's failures or resting on one's laurels in equal measure. It renews the opportunity to establish an honorable tradition. It makes each day a new beginning.

33. *CHUGI—LOYALTY*

One loyal friend is worth ten thousand relatives.

—Latin proverb

Carved on the scabbard of the master's *aikuchi* in picture form was the story of *Chushingura*, "The Forty-Seven Faithfuls." According to this ancient story, a young *daimyo* named Asano, having been insulted by another courtier named Kira, made the mistake of drawing his sword within the walls of Edo Castle. To atone for this transgression, the Shogun required that Lord Asano offer up his life. Well aware that they would be under strict observation in anticipation of retaliation, Asano's loyal retainers publicly disavowed their former lord and became *ronin*, "wave men," wandering the country and devolving into dissolute lifestyles. After sufficient time had passed, they secretly reassembled, and casting aside all pretense, stormed the castle of their master's adversary to exact their revenge, delivering Kira's severed head to Asano's grave. Having avenged their daimyo's death in violation of their duty to the Shogun, they too committed *seppuku* en masse. Their deeds are widely accepted as the paradigm of fidelity in Japanese culture.

In the martial sphere loyalty to one's superiors—the master, the dojo, and the ryu—is expected of the student. What is less well understood, however, is the concomitant and reciprocal duty owed by seniors to their juniors. They are obliged to provide assistance and protection. However inconvenient, arduous, or embarrassing they may be, these mutual obligations cannot be viewed as a sometimes thing. To be of any value, loyalty must be absolute. Like the teacher who takes on responsibility for his students, an exchange of loyalties binds the participants together inextricably. Thus, special care should be taken before committing oneself in this fashion.

An offer of loyalty can be for a specific matter or for all purposes. Paradoxically, the latter kind can be somewhat easier to maintain. Along the way, with a measure of luck, one will encounter kindred spirits of like sensibilities. Such people are to be treasured, and unconditional support afforded to them. The journey will be made easier and more pleasant by their company. Somewhat more problematic, however, is the situation in which one's loyalty is sought or requested by a relative stranger—a patient, a client, or an acquaintance perhaps. Refusing this request may not be a viable option, but neither should acceptance be granted lightly. What follows may present an ethical dilemma. You may not like what you hear. But once given, the commitment cannot and should not be withdrawn. This was the master's teaching.

34. *ICHIGO, ICHIE* — THE POWER OF ONE

One man with courage is a majority.

—Thomas Jefferson

The philosophy of one of Britain's greatest living Arctic explorers is predicated on the belief that one person can make a difference. Perhaps more so than its Eastern counterpart, the Western martial tradition is replete with examples of the power of one. Thomas Macaulay's epic poem tells the story of the Roman hero, Horatius, who single-handedly held back the mighty army of Lars Porsena for the better part of a day while the city's engineers destroyed the supporting beams of the last narrow bridge into the city on which Horatius stood and fought. Similarly, recent cinematic epics have shed new light on the individual courage of such highland heroes as Rob Roy MacGregor and William Wallace.

In a different vein, the quest to explore our world, particularly *Terra Australis Incognita*, "the Antarctic," has been advanced by a variety of singular individuals. In 1520, while sailing through the strait that bears his name, Magellan speculated that the land to his south, Tierra del Fuego, might mark the northern edge of a great continent. In 1578, during his voyage through the South American islands aboard the *Golden Hind*, Sir Francis Drake determined that the Great Southern Continent must lie even farther to the South. In February 1775, Captain James Cook completed the first circumnavigation of Antarctica.

Perhaps inspired by the example of these great explorers, Sir Robert Falcon Scott embarked on a heroic bid for the South Pole aboard the *Terra Nova* on November 29, 1910. On January 17, 1912, at 1830 hours, Scott arrived at the South Pole, only to find that his chief competitor, Roald Amundsen, had erected the Norwegian flag at the pole a month before. None of Scott's party survived the return trip, but his journal provides a testament to the courage of his men and an account of the singular sacrifice of the one for the greater good of the many.[3]

Seventy-five years later, moved by the story of Scott's ill-fated expedition to Antarctica, another great explorer determined to follow in his footsteps. This man has gone on to lead international expeditions to both poles, securing a place for himself in the history books and receiving the Order of the British Empire for his heroism. The truly remarkable thing about the man, however, is not his courage, his leadership, or his endurance. It is his motive. He does not do this for the sake of fame or financial gain. The purpose of his quest is to educate the youth of tomorrow about the fragile nature of the last great wilderness and humankind's collective responsibility to future generations.

---

3. Scott writes, "He said, 'I am just going outside and may be some time.' He went into the blizzard, and we have not seen him since. We knew that poor Oates was walking to his death; but, though we tried to dissuade him, we knew it was the act of a brave man and an English gentleman."—*Diary of Sir Robert Falcon Scott*

One day a student of the master who had also been a member of the explorer's polar team returned to the dojo. He brought with him a copy of a book detailing one of the Arctic expeditions, as a gift. The master was delighted. While he knew almost nothing of polar exploration, he recognized in the story a consonance of ideals, a kinship of spirit. As he paged through the photographs of the frozen landscape on a lazy autumn afternoon in the English countryside, for a moment, two cultures, two disciplines, and two masters became one. Then it was time to leave, and the spell was broken.

Ichigo, ichie, an expression commonly used in *chado,* "the way of tea," means "one encounter, one opportunity." Only rarely do the forces of time, place, and opportunity coalesce in perfect harmony. Such occurrences are to be treasured. They are also to be sought out and savored. For every ten ideas, five will likely fail, and four may falter. But the realization of the one is what makes the other attempts worthwhile. Regret at failure is as nothing when compared with remorse at never having tried at all. And the power of the one is truly something magical to behold.

35. *YAMAINU* — OF PACKS AND LONE WOLVES

There's a whiff of the lynch mob or the lemming migration about any overlarge concentration of like-thinking individuals, no matter how virtuous their cause.

—P. J. O'Rourke

To a staunch traditionalist or perhaps a member of the armed forces, the atmosphere of the dojo might have seemed undisciplined at times, particularly in the early days. It was never raucous or frenetic, but a certain looseness of structure was there, owing at least in part to the fact that the master was sparing with his words and the volume at which those words were spoken. When he had some necessary instruction to deliver, he never raised his voice to be heard. He did not have to. The punishment for not listening carefully was that you might not hear what he said.

Despite his powerful appearance and commanding persona—perhaps because of them—he conducted himself with deference and restraint at all times, as though the world was not capable of absorbing anything more than a small fraction of the intensity within. He wielded his power lightly. In truth, the students rarely tested him on this point, and the more senior practitioners were quick to snap back any newcomer who got out of line, but the line in question was not a bright one. There were very few "thou shalts" or "though shalt nots . . ." The required etiquette was of a subtler kind.

Under such circumstances, it might have been tempting to grow complacent, to assume that the old dog had no teeth, and to adopt a more lackadaisical approach to the matters being studied in that surreal environment, but every once in a while, a flash of white fangs served to remind the pack of the order of things. Such moments rarely involved any type of overt confrontation. It was more of a kind of change in the atmosphere as when the sun passes behind a dark cloud and the ambient heat and light levels drop precipitously. A look here and a swift movement there, just enough to alert those in the room that conditions had changed.

There were other signs too. The way he would sometimes stop in midsentence or movement and prick up his ears, straining to hear something that the others could not. Then having satisfied himself, he would resume the interrupted activity, hardly bothering to glance up when the interloper he had first detected finally trudged across the threshold. Or the look in his eye when one or other of the students failed to respond to a command appropriately or performed a technique well below the range of his abilities. He did not have to say or do anything else. The message was invariably received and understood.

As time went on, it became clear that this too was part of

the testing process. It would probably have been far easier and more efficient to run the dojo like a military barracks, demanding total silence unless addressed directly and wielding absolute power. Certainly not a man in the place had the will or the ability to oppose him. And that would have sufficed— but only for a season. For his goal was not to produce foot soldiers capable of executing his every command. His mission was to mold warriors, to shape men with the skill to fight, but the wisdom to know when to do so. And this could not be achieved within the rigid confines of a parade square. His saplings needed air and room to grow. Only in this way could he see the shape they were taking and prune them accordingly.

36. *HANARE*—TIME TO LET GO

It is the moment when flint and iron combine to create a spark.

—Kyudo kuden

For many archers, the most elusive skill in the hassetsu is *hanare*, "the release." Morikawa Kozan's seminal writings on this subject hang in kyudojo around the world. The decision to loose the arrow is not made by the archer, but by the bow and the arrow. It should be like snow slipping from a leaf in the morning sun. The sword already knows how to cut and the bow how to shoot. The artist's job is merely to stay out of the way. So is it in life. Circumstances will indicate when it is time to let go. No amount of agitation can expedite the process; no amount of lingering can delay it. One can always insist on being early or late, but the appointed hour comes and goes of its own accord.

The secret, then, is to make every effort to be ready for the moment when it arrives. Plan, certainly, but as the master teaches, remain flexible, for fate follows no mortal timetable.

The enlightened warrior remains open to the signs from all quarters. There is a pattern to things for those who choose to see it. They appreciate each stage to the best of their ability, but remain ready. In the space between two heartbeats, it will be time to move on.

**PART
FOUR**

Harmony

37. *NATSUKUSAYA*—THE WARRIOR'S DREAM

Oh, the summer grasses/All that remains/Of a young warrior's dreams?
No! Two travelers/On the narrow Way to a far province.

—Matsuo Basho

The master was a model of patience, requiring very little in the way of natural talent or speed of progress from his students. He once explained that, unlike some of his own classmates, the knowledge and skill had not come easily for him. Perhaps these shortcomings had helped to make him a better

133

teacher. But there were times when, despite his best efforts to conceal it, his disappointment was apparent. His eyes would seem to lose their focus momentarily. Tiny crow's feet would pull at either side. And a thin, flat, forced smile would take the place of some more natural expression. At times like this, it was hard to say who felt more embarrassment, teacher or student.

Apart from this minor example, however, negative emotions simply did not seem to be part of his makeup. Within the dojo and without, even his senior students could not recall ever having seen him angry or sad (and the idea of the master being afraid of anything was quite simply laughable). It would not be quite accurate to describe him as upbeat or cheery, but he always projected an air of contentment. For this reason, the single instance of melancholy in those many years remained poignant.

Summer had come and gone, taking with it fond memories of punting on the river and practicing in the grass, and the Michaelmas term had not yet begun. The university and the finishing school were both on holiday, and no classes were scheduled at either location. Nevertheless, one of the students of both institutions had nowhere else to go and decided to use the free day to take some photographs of the remarkable Japanese architecture that lay hidden in the wooded glade at the end of a winding lane. He took the train to the nearest station and completed the journey on foot, down narrow country lanes with high hedges as he had so many times before. But this time was different.

An eerie stillness seemed to have settled over the land. The normally bustling schools stood empty, and a recent change in the weather had signaled the departure of the last of the holidaymakers, leaving a palpable silence in their wake. It seemed that no one was on the road today, and even the railway carriage had delivered the photographer to his destination in solitude. No birds sang. It was as though this little piece of the English countryside had somehow been pulled from the slipstream of time and frozen in place.

As the student approached the stone markers that guarded the wooded entranceway, he could hear his own breathing and feel his heart beating in his chest. It was overcast, and the uncooperative weather, together with the unnerving loneliness, had almost made him abort his mission and plan to come again another day. But now that he was here, perhaps just a few pictures before returning to the relative warmth and safety of his little flat and the four-station, black-and-white television next to the electric fire.

He snapped a shot of the stone guardians, and then moved on beneath the tall canopy of gently shedding trees, gravel crunching loudly beneath the soles of his boots. He made his way to the archery range and took another shot from the firing point looking down toward the targets. Still he had not seen a soul. The last shot he wanted was one of the traditional building with the pagoda-style roof that housed the dojo. As he took this final picture, the student thought he heard a noise coming from within.

With infinite care he eased open the heavy outer door and stole inside. He followed the sound down the familiar hallway to the inner door of the dojo. It stood ajar. As he peered through the crack, he saw the unmistakable silhouette of the master. Dressed in street clothes, the old man was wandering through the abandoned hall, tidying here, polishing there, all the while singing and mumbling to himself. From this new vantage point, he looked somehow smaller—and sad. The student was about to knock when he heard his teacher's voice break. He could not make out many of the words, but the last phrase stuck in his head. *"Yume no ato . . ."* The younger man turned without a sound and made his way back home as quietly as he had come.

Natsu Kusa

Natsukusa ya,	*Oh, the summer grasses,*
Tsuwamono domo ga	*All that remains*
Yume no ato?	*Of a young warrior's dreams?*
Ie! Doshi imas ni	*No! Two travelers*
Oku no hosomichi	*On the narrow Way to a far province.*

—*Matsuo Basho*

38. *THE DAO—*
INTERCONNECTEDNESS

All strangers are relations to each other.

—Arabian proverb

To a Western mindset, Eastern theories of healing or of harming can make very little intuitive sense. Practitioners of traditional Chinese medicine are not as concerned with the patient's case history as with his current mood, coloring, and gastronomic preferences. The master of kyusho-jutsu can find relationships among the five elements of the *gogyo* in virtually any combination of techniques rather than adhering strictly to the simplistic patterns of the generating and controlling cycles. The *roshi*'s response to virtually any question is another question or, on those rare occasions when he allows himself to be pinned down to some degree, "It depends."

These nonlinear approaches all have their foundation in

Oriental cosmology. In the Western conception, occurrences are thought to be related sequentially—*post hoc ergo procter hoc*. In the Eastern view, however, events are linked by virtue of concurrency. Being born in the year of a particular animal, for example, will imbue the child with a measure of the character of that creature. Until recently, Western science has given short shrift to the notion that such discrete phenomena can have an instantaneous effect on one another. With the advent of subatomic theory and the chaos paradigm, however, Western minds are opening to this concept.

Feng shui (the art of wind and water) is predicated on the notion that there is both a connection and a relationship among all things. Some call this the interconnectedness. According to its teachings, there is a preferred location, direction, angle, and orientation for each thing, relative to every other. In the layout of a home, for example, one particular school of Eastern geomancy instructs that there should be mountains to the north, open fields to the south, a road to the west, and water to the east. Careful consideration of the prevailing practicalities in the time and place of this art's genesis, including wind patterns, geographic features, and strategic considerations, reveals this to have been a remarkably practical rule of thumb.

The *I Ching* (the *Book of Changes*) may be seen as a dynamic manifestation of this sincere belief in the interconnectedness. Rather than contemplating the location of objects relative to one another, the *I Ching* focuses more on the relationships between people. Based on the interactions of the eight trigrams, the book has been used in Eastern cultures for centuries as a tool of prognostication as well as a source of guidance. A fairly direct connection between these principles and the martial arts exists in the practices of Bagua and Xing I, internal Chinese disciplines, which together with T'ai

Chi compose the so-called Wu Tang arts. At an advanced level, each of these styles relies at least in part on the principles of proper placement as they relate to the symbology of the eight trigrams.

The master suggested, as he was wont to do, that there was a deeper truth to be grasped herein. Over time, he coaxed from his students the realization that if all things truly were interconnected, it provided the initiate with a powerful tool for constructive or destructive purposes. In either case, however, it required the participation of another. There had to be at least two.

39. *DOCERE VERSUS DUCERE—*
INSTRUCTORS AND EDUCATORS

I hear, I forget. I see, I remember. I do, I understand.

—Confucius

To instruct is to show. The focus is on the instructor. To educate is to bring out. The focus is on the student. An instructor imparts knowledge. An educator allows the student to perform what he knows and makes minor adjustments along the way. Thus, while instruction thrives on the instructor demonstrating his superior knowledge, education flourishes in an atmosphere of encouragement and tolerance. Instruction is intrusive and dictatorial. Education is detached and communal. The true educator understands that the process is no longer about him. Use of the Socratic method is education. Lecture format is mere teaching. Either the martial spirit dwells in the student or it does not. It may be teased out and cultivated. It cannot be transplanted or imported.

Those who choose to instruct rather than to educate also tend to say rather than to do. The Chinese proverb tells us that it is not the cry, but the flight of the wild bird that leads the flock to follow. In addition to expediting the learning process and ensuring that the students actually break a sweat, preferring action to words serves another valuable purpose: it prevents the teacher from devolving into an armchair warrior or, in the Japanese idiom, from beginning to smell of old leaves. There is a tendency among novices to deify their teachers. Sadly, some instructors will readily accept this and begin even to believe it. One of the master's cardinal rules was that the teacher may give advice, but he should never allow the substitution of his will for the student's own.

Teachers who choose to instruct rather than to educate tend to lecture rather than to discuss. Remaining on the distant side of the notional boundary between master and student, they rely on the assistance of one or two senior apprentices, thereby precluding any meaningful interaction with the student body at large. They fail to appreciate the individuality of their charges and deny them the possibility of engaging with their teacher in a meaningful fashion. They also risk putting their students to sleep. This is the way of mass production. It is not Kishido. Education is an organic and self-sustaining process that relies on the student's innate abilities. Without constant attention, by contrast, mere instruction will wither and fade away. In the fullness of time, the disciple will graduate and walk the path alone, at least for a season. When an instructor is gone, the student can only cast his mind back and try to emulate the example. When an educator is gone, the apprentice's own abilities remain, with the educator's corrections echoing in his ears. In this way teacher and student become one; master and disciple are united. The tradition is not merely preserved; it lives on.

40. *PRIMUM EST NON NOCERE—* FIRST DO NO HARM

A statement once let loose cannot be caught by four horses.

—Japanese proverb

As he grew older, the master began to turn the supervision of the testing process over to certain senior students. Among them was one with a particularly sharp tongue. At the conclusion of a grueling test, this assistant summarily informed a particular candidate that he had failed. When the master learned of this, he was not pleased. It was not clear whether he took issue with the substance or the manner of delivery of the harsh judgment, but to that senior's great shame, he publicly reversed the decision. When asked about this event at a later time, he explained that the assistant's behavior had violated one of the cardinal principles of Kishido—do no harm.

In the space of one breath, a teacher can turn an impressionable student away from a particular discipline, or even the arts in general, for all time. It takes only a single instance of poor judgment to make such a blunder. In the final analysis, the damage done by such thoughtless behavior must be weighed against every superb technique and stellar student produced over a lifetime of teaching. According to the master, the observation of some simple rules can serve to prevent such a tragedy. Be kind. Be patient. Maintain a professional distance. Do not become romantically involved with students. Think before speaking.

A subtler blight can also stunt the growth of vulnerable saplings. It is the resort to generalized negativity. While an unusually harsh word can snap off a limb, constant criticism causes withering in the tree as a whole. It creates the impression that no amount of effort will result in progress. It is a philosophy of hopelessness. The master's approach was to find something, anything, that the student could do correctly and build upon it. Forging layer upon layer in a constructive effort will generally yield a sturdier result than hacking away at a chunk of raw material in a destructive fashion. For those to whom the idea of positive reinforcement is a novelty, it might be wise to work with junipers for a time, before taking on students. Or fig trees—they are hardier.

41. *CHACUN À SON GOÛT*—HORSES FOR COURSES

Live your own life, for you will surely die your own death.

—Latin proverb

Quite apart from one's profession, each person has a calling, a spiritual idiom most aptly suited to his nature. Some are followers; some are leaders. Some are healers, teachers, warriors, or poets at heart, regardless of the manner in which they choose to make their living. Considerable difficulty can be avoided by discovering this truth early on and adapting to its particular contours. To struggle against the forces of nature is a futile and sometimes risky business.

It was the master's practice to identify each student with the particular animal that best represented his spirit. He would, of course, encourage each one to strive to expand his armamentarium, to diversify his martial portfolio, but always he was mindful of the dangers implicit in trying to mold the student into something he was not.

In the *Book of Five Rings*, Musashi likens men to types of wood and the strategist to the master carpenter. He urges consideration of the strength, durability, and finish of each piece relative to the task at hand. The construction of a house requires many different types of lumber—vast load-bearing beams and ornate cornices, sturdy floorboards, and rich, dark paneling. The artisan's skill lies in recognizing the appropriate material, finishing it skillfully, installing it properly, and wasting none.

Apart from the inherent appeal of this judicious and economical approach, it fosters the prospect that the student may one day surpass the teacher. If every follower strives to conform to the same archetype, it denies the possibility of evolution, innovation, and beneficial mutation. If each one's aim is no higher than his predecessor's, many will fall short of the mark, and even the best will proceed no further than those who have gone before. There will be no progress, and without forward motion, stagnation will occur.

42. *SHOJIN*—DEMAGOGUES AND CURMUDGEONS

We make a living by what we get, we make a life by what we give.

—Sir Winston Churchill

The master's approach to the sensitive issue of financial matters, as illustrated by his tale of the itinerant monk and the bowl, has already been discussed. In the matter of the master's storytelling, however, the fact that he would laugh at its conclusion is at least as important as the lesson itself. In addition to those teachers who are motivated by a hunger for money, there are also those who are driven by a thirst for power. They bask in the limelight that their office, and not their person, commands. They surround themselves with younger, more impressionable, less experienced people, in a vainglorious effort to appear the more impressive by contrast. And while their subordinates inevitably progress and surpass them, they themselves remain mired. They are like the morbidly obese man wearing vertical stripes, hoping to benefit from the slimming effect, or the college sophomore returning to his high school in search of a date.

For novices to focus the vast majority of their attention on their own progress along a path is entirely appropriate. Like all beginners, they must take care to ensure that inexperience does not cause them to falter. The more seasoned traveler, and certainly any good leader, by contrast, has both the ability and the inclination to look out for the well-being of fellow travelers and to consider the trail itself. It is, indeed, this very lack of self-consciousness that betokens acumen, expertise, and poise. Those who maintain an introspective focus long after having achieved sufficient proficiency to do otherwise, declare their immaturity. They also miss many beautiful opportunities along the way.

Particularly after having achieved a degree of competence, the student's studies and abilities must serve some greater purpose. In ancient times, the samurai trained to serve his lord. In fact, the very word samurai (like the term sergeant) derives from a root meaning "to serve." In the modern era, with the exception of a few vocations, this is no longer the case. It is selfish to study merely for one's own benefit. It is also empty. A person must dedicate his effort to a cause, whether it be the education of students, the preservation of tradition, the championing of a particular philosophy, or the act of doing something *pro bono publico*, "for the public good." To campaign merely in the interests of one's own self—this is not the Way of the Western Warrior.

The misguided often seek to detract from potential competitors to perpetuate a focus on the self. Like any alpha male, they will snarl and glare at a perceived rival and slink off to sulk or curry favor if a direct confrontation seems imprudent.

But humanity is not a wolf pack, or at least it should not be. Such behavior is base and callow and has no place in a civilized society. The arrival of a competitor of similar stature should evoke a positive reaction; one finds few pleasures greater than discussing a mutual interest with one's equal. At a minimum, etiquette requires that one refrain from injecting negativity into the situation.

Each of us chooses, by and large, the tinting of the lenses through which the world is viewed. For some inexplicable reason, certain people prefer a dismal shade of gray, distorted by bad-tempered scratch marks. There are other ways than this. Ill humor is no substitute for sincerity.

In seeking the appropriate balance in many realms, the master advised, "More than a week, less than a year." Even an ox can set his horns and charge at an obstacle until one or other of them yields. It takes wisdom and judgment to know when and where to strike, for maximum effect with minimum effort. It is also more elegant. Like the pilot flaring (a maneuver to lower speed) just before touchdown, low enough to prevent a stall, but high enough to avoid simply driving the aircraft onto the runway, there is a balance to be sought, a harmony to be achieved. So in one's martial practice. Ideally, it is more than a hobby, but less than a cult.

43. *STARE DECISIS*—TRADITION

Never regard study as a duty, but as the enviable
opportunity to learn to know the liberating influence of
beauty in the realm of the spirit for your own personal
joy and to the profit of the community to which your
later work belongs.

—Albert Einstein

Few traditional dojos do not have a *shinza*, or shrine, at the
kamiza, but there are many who misunderstand the purpose
of this custom, thinking it akin to an orthodox religious altar.
Religion or spirituality is a somewhat more flexible concept
in the East. For example, a common practice in Japan is to
adhere to Shinto tenets in early life, but shift the emphasis to
Buddhist practices later. Similarly, many Japanese rooms
boast a tokonoma, but, according to the master, to equate this
concept with an altar in the Western sense of the word is to

misunderstand the matter entirely. The shelves that are positioned on the front wall of many schools of the martial arts, and the objects that they display, are perhaps best thought of as a memorial.

The study of a traditional art emphasizes both the practical and customary value of maintaining a link with those who have gone before. The crusades of the past masters provide education, inspiration, and assurance that their teachings have been battle tested and refined by the passage of time. For this reason the oral tradition is very much alive in training halls around the world. The ancient legends and parables are instructive, and if they also happen to be true, so much the better (or, to paraphrase Trevanian, they are statements so true that they do not have to be real).

Treading a martial path is made easier by looking to the tracks of those who have passed this way before. If each traveler had to plot his course anew through undiscovered country and break trail for the first time, taking dead ends and circumnavigating obstacles, no progress could be made beyond the span of one person's lifetime. Rather, each new generation builds upon the work of the last. It is a cooperative

venture. What seems an obvious shortcut at present was once nothing more than a bold idea and the determination to see it through.

There will inevitably come a time when a particular route proves impassable and must be abandoned. This should be done, however, with respect and a due sense of regret and not accompanied by bitterness and vocal condemnation. It is a matter of honoring tradition. It is a gesture of deference to the pioneers. It is the reason that courtesy should always be given first to shinza.

44. *GIREI* — PROFESSIONAL COURTESY

The true spirit of conversation consists in building on another man's observation, not overturning it.

—Edward Bulwer-Lytton

The story is told to novices of the young practitioner who approached a particular master of the martial arts and informed him that another instructor had stolen some of his techniques and was teaching them in his own classes. Mirroring the student's conspiratorial demeanor, this true gentleman leaned in closer and whispered, "That's all right. I steal his techniques too. . . . We call it, 'sharing.'"

There is a tradition in the professions of extending particular courtesy to one's peers. Doctors who have never made a house call in their lives will often treat an ailing colleague at the latter's convenience. Attorneys, a generally rancorous bunch, will typically come together when one of their number is threatened. While it would be encouraging to see this spirit of civility extend beyond emergent situations, at least these remnants of a bygone age endure after a fashion. Sadly, the same cannot always be said of the martial community at large. While there may be a certain predisposition to conflict inherent in the study of a martial way, steps should be taken to ensure that the spirit of combat remains properly confined to the dojo in all but the most extreme circumstances.

Another story from the oral tradition contrasts the skill of three brothers trained in the art of healing. One was capable of curing severe illnesses, pulling patients back from the brink of death. As a result of his spectacular successes, his name was known throughout the land. The second could arrest the progress of a disease before it became acute, and consequently, his reputation only extended as far as the county line. The eldest could detect the seeds of the malady in an ostensibly healthy person and, thereby, prevent the occurrence of the pathology in the first place. His abilities, therefore, were only known to his patients themselves.

Extending this model beyond the medical sphere leads to the conclusion that the best attorney should strive to prevent litigation, and the progressive peace officer should strive to prevent crime. According to the master, the enlightened warrior should seek to eliminate conflict. One way to foster civility in the martial community is to extend a measure of professional courtesy to one's colleagues. One may not agree with or even condone the practices of one's peers, but to resort to public bickering lowers the tone of the profession as a whole. Think twice before airing an opinion, especially if it is an unhelpful one.

45. *KIKI* — OPPORTUNITY

When I'm working on a problem, I never think about
beauty. I think only how to solve the problem. But
when I have finished, if the solution is not beautiful,
I know it is wrong.

—R. Buckminster Fuller

The samurai used his obi as a kind of medieval utility belt.
Its multiple layers allowed for daisho to be worn without their
saya rubbing against each other. The folds that lay across the
front of the belly could be used to hold *sensu*, *tanto*, or *washi*.

In the master's tradition, aikuchi is worn transversely
across the back, but he was often seen carrying a length of
wood about the size of a knife in the front of his obi. When
asked about this item, he explained that it was the *tsuka* of
his first *bokken*, a length of white oak that had shattered during vigorous *kumitachi*. At first, he had considered discarding
the apparently useless item, but had later taken to carrying it

with him when it would have been inconvenient or otherwise improper to wear a full-length sword. In time he had developed the ability to "see" the rest of the blade, extending outward from this remnant, and, thereby, gained the ability to practice his sword forms no matter where he found himself. In difficulty he had found opportunity. His students referred to this item as his light saber, thereafter.

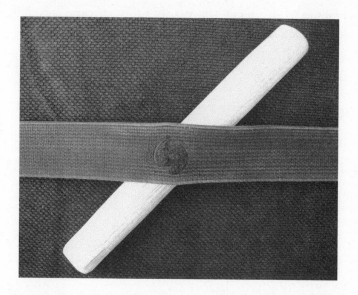

No matter how carefully one proceeds along the path, problems will inevitably arise. Adoption of a steady pace is likely to distribute these occurrences sufficiently far apart to allow for a measured response. Reacting to such upsets with annoyance tends to aggravate the situation as well as the protagonist. The ancient saying reminds us that the character for crisis contains the symbol for opportunity. The value of this cliché can be realized by deciding that grappling with a problem should be coupled with an effort to better the status quo.

Rather than temporarily patching a leak, replace the pipe with a stronger one. Carry a book at all times so that an unanticipated delay turns into a chance to get caught up on some reading. Turn an inadvertent mark into a beautiful decoration.

While this is not always possible, it is a useful and positive exercise at least to look for possibilities in unexpected and frequently unwelcome occurrences. Results will vary from total failure to surprising success. But the outcome is collateral to the objective—welcoming opportunity.

46. *KOUHEI*—NO ONE IS ABOVE THE LAW

To win one hundred victories in one hundred battles is not the acme of skill. To subdue the enemy without fighting is the acme of skill.

—Sun Tzu

The British system of government does not enjoy the same distinct bifurcation of legislative and executive authority as its American counterpart. The influence of the royal family no longer operates to balance the prime minister's power in any real sense. This system, therefore, has evolved another manner of regulating the policies of the members of parliament in the form of the civil servants, known as mandarins, as a result of their official longevity. Moreover, these "secretaries" can delay, discourage, and dissuade even the most determined elected official from his preferred course of action with such finesse that the victim rarely suspects the true source of his frustration.

Lord Acton's famous observation regarding the corruptive nature of power underscores the dangers as much to an individual as to a nation. For what is political science but psychology on a national level? In any hierarchy there exists the potential for abuse, and nowhere is this concern more present than the master-student relationship. Disciples often look to their teachers as the source of all wisdom, particularly in the context of the martial arts. An extraordinary strength of character is needed to avoid the seduction of such adulation.

The surest way to keep away from temptation is to hold oneself to a higher standard and to avoid even the appearance of impropriety. The didactic dynamic is already weighted in favor of the teacher. The teacher is the one who decides the subject matter, the mode of communication, and the parameters of training. Too often, an instructor will cover bad technique with excessive force or retrofit a result to make it seem as though that was his purpose all along, in effect calling the shot after the ball was sunk. These tendencies proceed from an unwillingness to admit error, which is to say, humanity.

The master had a strict prohibition on the use of profanity in the dojo. Not to say that such language offended his delicate sensibilities, but rather that he felt such conduct was unbecoming and was indicative of a loss of control and a poor attitude. Any such exclamation during an examination resulted in instant failure, and he had been known to assign a student as many as a thousand push-ups on the eve of a test, to ensure that one day's indiscretion did not carry over into the next.

Late one evening, after practice had ended, and the dojo was otherwise deserted, a lone novice was washing the tatami, while the master pulled yajiri from the *makiwara*. For reasons unknown, the latter suddenly exclaimed, *"Shimatta"*— a mild expletive. The student thought nothing of it until he had made his final bow to shinza before heading off in the direction of the railway station, and heard the master's voice counting out his own punitive repetitions from inside the darkened dojo: *"Ich . . . ni . . . san . . ."*

47. *ON*—INTO THE FOLD

The spirit in which a thing is given determines that in which the debt is acknowledged; it's the intention, not the face-value of the gift, that's weighed.

—Seneca

The arrival of the big Russian was a cause of consternation for some. Tall and powerfully built, he had dropped to the floor in a perfect split at the beginning of his first class, although he had no formal training in the martial arts. It had not taken long for him to secure an invitation to the master's dojo, where he continued to impress. The problem was this: There were several in the school who had worked very hard for the knowledge and skill they had obtained and for the respect and seniority they had earned from their master and their colleagues. This newcomer threatened to upset that equilibrium with his overabundance of natural gifts.

As was typically the case, initial supervision of the new

recruit fell to a handful of senior students. Unified against this common enemy, both Eastern and Western assistants worked hard to make sure the Russian knew his place—and theirs as well. He was a favorite when it came time to choosing opponents for sparring, rarely if ever sitting out a "dance." And while no serious injury ever resulted, it was more a testament to his armored hide than to any restraint being exhibited by his opponents in the ring. Off the mat, the linguistic and cultural divide was more an excuse than a reason for the lack of warmth they showed him.

Nevertheless, the newcomer kept coming back, week after week, perhaps hoping that sheer heart could win over his hostile peers. Judging by the tenor of the sparring matches, his commitment was having the opposite effect. And yet at the end of every class, he always managed a cheerful smile and an enthusiastic farewell. Things might have improved on their own, or they might have deteriorated. It is hard to say because, as on so many other occasions, just a few words from the master changed the perspective for everyone in the blink of an eye.

After one of the more grueling sparring classes, the master asked his seniors to remain behind. As they sat at his feet in a semicircle, he explained that each new student who was admitted to the tradition took on a debt to those who had gone before. This debt was not measured in anything as base as money. Rather, it was carried by the practitioner along the way until the time came when he encountered another kindred spirit and brought that person into the fold. It was the highest goal of any teacher, he explained, to forge a student whose abilities exceeded his own. Only then would the obligation be satisfied. For now there would be two companions walking the narrow road to a far province.

48. *TATSUTORIATOWONIGOSAZU* — LEAVE THINGS A LITTLE BETTER THAN YOU FOUND THEM

We do not inherit the earth from out parents. We borrow it from our children.

—Native American proverb

There is a communal tradition in the Outward Bound program that allows travelers, particularly in remote and hostile areas, to take shelter and sustenance from any of the occasional outposts along the way, but it requires them to leave something in exchange. No one is ever quite sure how these cabins and campsites got there in the first place—they rarely appear on any map. Yet there they stand, unlocked and unguarded, but always tidy, well stocked, and free from vandalism. Depleted provisions can be replenished, but it is expected that some excess supplies will be left in their place. Firewood and water should be restocked and order restored before breaking camp the next day.

The master honored this tradition in his own fashion. When notebooks were submitted for evaluation, they would always be returned with some additional material. He once borrowed a *jo* staff from a student for a demonstration, re-turning it some days later—deep polishing had brought out a hitherto undiscovered luster in the dark wood. He did these things as a matter of course. While he never articulated this principle explicitly, it was clear that he expected the same from his students. He taught by example. It was a necessary part of Kishido.

**PART
FIVE**

Void

49. *KOTAN* — ELEGANT SIMPLICITY

Pass through knowledge to arrive at simplicity.

—Trevanian

A gentle breeze carried the scent of the wolf pack downwind to a meadow where a cat and fox sat talking. "Wolves," the fox nonchalantly remarked. "I know a thousand ways to get away from them." He was very boastful and began enumerating all his various evasion tactics.

By and by the cat, who had just climbed the tree, called down, "I only know one," but it was too late—the pack had fallen on the fox and he could no longer hear.

Many of the master's students supposed that his custom of

practicing some of the most basic techniques before class was intended for their benefit, by way of example. They were constantly being told to begin with *kihon*, "fundamentals," as opposed to the more sophisticated and intriguing advanced waza. Yet on more than one occasion, the master's wife confirmed that even when he trained alone, the repetition of these simple movements was what occupied the majority of his time.

Once a student has absorbed the essential elements of a technique, little can be said or written to distinguish its execution from that of a master. Yet even to the uninitiated, the difference between the two performances is pronounced. It is something that must really be seen or felt to be understood. There is a grace, a depth, and a character to the movements of the expert, akin to the fit of a well broken in pair of boots. While the student and the master may seem to be running side by side on the track, this clearly occurs because one has lapped the other.

Most kenjutsu-ka are familiar with the practice of performing a painfully high number of repetitions of a single waza with a heavy practice *suburito* so as to allow fatigue and dis-

comfort to sand down the corners of their technique, eliminating extraneous movements. The resulting economy of movement, applied to all things, begins to hint at the principle of *kotan*. What some might mistake for a casual affect is merely relaxation born of experience and confidence. It is certainly not indicative of inattentiveness.

The reciprocal aspect of this principle dictates a heightened state of perception at other times. The level of focus does not change, merely the background. Where the novice might concentrate on a technique with such intensity that he chokes its effectiveness, only to trip over a pair of *zori* on his way out of the dojo, the master's awareness remains constant. He will open a window or pour a cup of tea with the same elegant simplicity that sets his kata apart from all others.

50. *HEISEI* — SERENITY

When you hear the splash/of the water drops that
fall/into the stone bowl/you will feel that all the
dust/of your mind is washed away.

—Sen-No-Rikyu

A visit to the master's cottage was always an enlightening experience. At first, the main objective, as in the dojo, was merely to avoid making any inadvertent faux pas. There were many things to be remembered: shoes should be left at the threshold, toes pointed toward the door; *seiza* and *anza* are the only permissible sitting positions; and the sole of the foot must never be exposed in the direction of another. In time, the observation of these formalities became second nature, and it was possible to concentrate more fully on the intricacies of imperfect bilingual conversation. Eventually, the students were even able to divide their attention between understanding through listening and learning through observation. They stole

glances at the myriad treasures—scrolls, boxes, and seals—
that occupied the shelves in the master's study, and they
watched his every move intently.

The tenor of these visits was chiefly one of serenity. In retrospect, however, the architect of this atmosphere was not the
master himself, but his wife. She seemed to materialize at the
master's side from time to time, proffering the particular item
he was about to start looking for or supplying the correct
translation for a difficult concept without any air of superiority. She would come and go with such grace that her passage
was scarcely more noticeable than a soft breeze or a pleasant
aroma. She seemed to contain such an abundance of tranquility that the excess spilled over into these late evening sessions, like a soothing balm. It was not surprising to learn that
she was a practitioner of chado. She was a serene being.

The modern world is increasingly characterized by frenetic
activity. Noise pollution threatens to shatter the sound of
silence in much the same way that smog has begun to obscure

the stars. We wake up to the piercing shrill of an alarm. Car dealers shriek advertisements at us from the morning radio program. Our workday is disrupted by the insistent interjection of phone, fax, and e-mail. The unruly offspring of inconsiderate parents shatter the tranquility of a restaurant meal. Noisy neighbors, heavy traffic, and in some places, sirens and gunfire interrupt the evening hours.

The quest for a measure of stillness, both internal and external, is among the many reasons that people turn to a martial discipline. The minimalism of the dojo is a refreshing contrast to the excesses of the workaday world. Yet the master's wife ably demonstrated that such peacefulness does not reside exclusively within the martial province. Despite the increasing intrusiveness of exterior influences, one can and should still seek a measure of internal serenity. Like the deepsea diver, remember, one must pause for decompression once in a while during the ascent, to embrace the stillness of an action not taken and a secret left untold.

51. *FUGA*—REFINEMENT

Do not seek to follow in the footsteps of wise men, seek what they sought.

—Matsuo Basho

While the rest of the class struggled with the several alphabets of Japanese characters, the master painted the same symbol repeatedly—*enso*. To the untrained eye, each iteration appeared identical to the last—a single clockwise stroke producing a bold and symmetrical circle. Yet the master's expression betrayed a wide range of reactions to the evidently varying quality of his work. The ability to track the prescribed path with his brush was only the beginning. He was engaged in the pursuit of nuance, flavor, feeling. It was a process of gradual refinement.

Some schools of martial arts require absolute mastery of a particular concept before allowing progression to the next stage. Some kendo dojo teach the correct manner of breathing for a year or more, before even introducing the student to the *shinai*. Many kyudo sensei require months of practicing the hassetsu shaho in pantomime and then with *gomuyumi*, "a rubber practice bow," before allowing the archer access even to the makiwara. This is one end of the spectrum.

A frequent criticism of many students is that they seek to run before having learned to walk properly. They are so keen to penetrate the inner secrets of an art, that they fail to appreciate the importance of a solid foundation, without which oku are nothing more than a crown without a king. Many Western teachers of bujutsu have been criticized for the alacrity with which they introduce advanced and sometimes dangerous techniques, without having prepared their deshi, physically, mentally, or spiritually for the responsibility such knowledge entails. This is the other extreme.

Somewhere in between lies the master's way. His philosophy encouraged each student to progress exactly as quickly as he was able, no more and no less. Mindful of a host of considerations, the master would carefully select which technique to teach the student and when to teach it. It was a twofold process. As the student polished the technique, the master polished the student. The results are hardly surprising: no two pieces ever turned out quite the same.

The common thread throughout these divergent processes, however, was the inexorable progress toward a common goal—refinement. Do not block when you can lead. Do not lead when you can deflect. Do not deflect when you can evade. Do not evade when you can prevent. Refine.

52. *ENRYO*—RESERVE

When you talk of war, which no doubt would be
general war, you must not underrate England—she is
a curious country and few foreigners can understand
her mind. Do not judge by the attitude of the present
administration. Once a great cause is presented to
the people, all kinds of unexpected actions might
be taken.

—Sir Winston Churchill

There is a kata in the sequence known as *Hachiman*, in
which the swordsman lays down his blade and appears to ca-
pitulate. Should the opponent be discourteous enough to
continue his attack, however, the aikuchi, hitherto concealed
from sight, makes a swift rejoinder. The lesson here is reserve,
but according to the master, of two different varieties. Clearly,
the pattern illustrates the value of having a backup plan at all

times. But a deeper meaning emerges from the fact of the opening move—giving way to the adversary.

Many difficulties can be avoided by intervention at a sufficiently early stage. Sometimes, however, the appropriate solution is not to act, but to yield. This is a delicate matter that must be undertaken with some care. It is not proper to submit out of fear, fatigue, or laziness—such concession can scarcely be considered voluntary. Neither is obsequiousness or sycophancy to be encouraged. To step aside out of deference, courtesy, or philanthropy is appropriate and even admirable. In the words of President John Kennedy delivering his famous inaugural address, "Civility is not a sign of weakness."

The tactics of preemption and yielding find perhaps their most artful mode of expression in tandem. The art of modest, self-effacing understatement can prevent the escalation of tensions long before critical mass is achieved. Rather than vying for dominance like wolves in a pack, the gentleman-warrior should eschew such posturing and adopt a more reluctant approach to useless antagonism.

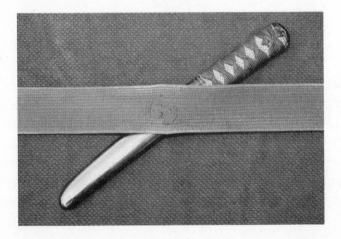

Holding back can serve a variety of purposes. Polygraphists and interrogators generally agree that a suspect will often reveal the truth if the examiner merely remains silent. In the martial community, as in life, those who feel the need to advertise their abilities and trumpet their successes from the rooftops are telling those with ears to hear that they are uncomfortable letting others make judgments for themselves, and must lobby hard to compensate for their deficiencies. Remember that the best dojo are generally hard to find and the finest teachers are too busy to be out soliciting additional students.

53. *PANACHE* — A WHITE PLUME

If a man insisted always on being serious, and never allowed himself a bit of fun and relaxation, he would go mad or become unstable without knowing it.

—Herodotus

The master's command of the English language, in combination with his students' embryonic Japanese, was sufficient for most purposes. It seemed strange, therefore, that his communication skills tended to break down entirely in the company of tiresome people. At times like this, he would murmur an incomprehensible apology and turn away and shake his head sadly, often with a surreptitious wink for any bemused onlooker.

To do great things without any zeal, passion, or flair is a terrible waste. It reduces the performer to the level of a machine, or a trained animal, or an actor, worse still. All good things are improved vastly by the injection of a modicum of style, and even the quite bad can be made tolerable thereby. And in most spheres of modern human endeavor—politics, law, medicine, and art—the plummeting decline of originality, finesse, and élan makes it relatively easy to shine by comparison. Consider the legacy of the past: the oratory of Churchill and Kennedy; the character of Wendell Holmes and Marshall; and the humor of Einstein. Whom can we offer in return?

The pilot who executes a flyby upon surviving a hazardous journey; the boxer who flicks his helpless opponent from the ropes rather than pummeling him into the canvas; the composer whose crescendo spills over unexpectedly into the minor mode; and the doctor who wears a monocle because spectacles are just too damned ordinary, these are men of style. There is also a certain appeal in the demeanor of the professor who thoughtfully pulls on his pipe while a cloud of smoke obscures the university's strict tobacco prohibition on the sign overhead or the deck sergeant who insists on waking his troops to Handel's "Water Music" instead of reveille. Victorian etiquette cautions that vulgarity is only permissible where it is also amusing. Similarly, mere ostentation and disobedience are of little value. Stylishness is of a more subtle nature. It requires a delicate balance, which one must judge for himself. It is also an important component in the Way of the Western Warrior. One way to begin is by making sure never to pass a puddle without splashing in it.

On his deathbed, Cyrano de Bergerac, Edmond Rostand's legendary master swordsman, looked not to past victories or to his true love, but to his white plume—his panache.

54. *HAKUHYO*—FIRE AND ICE

One ought never to turn one's back on a threatened
danger and try to run away from it. If you do that, you
will double the danger. But if you meet it promptly and
without flinching, you will reduce the danger by half.

—Winston Churchill

As has already been discussed, many schools of Japanese
archery require new students to practice the fundamental
eight positions of the archer over and over again with a rubber bow before allowing them even to touch a real weapon.
The master's approach was somewhat different. For the first
few weeks, he simply invited the novices to come along with
him to the shaho and observe as he and some of his senior
archers fired pair after pair of counterbalanced arrows down-
range. At first it was fascinating, seeing how shot after shot
would strike the heart of the mato, apparently with minimal
effort on the part of the shooter. But after a time, some of the

students began to grow restless watching the near identical performances, eager to get their own hands on a weapon.

No doubt aware of their flagging attention spans, the master explained that this was no mere spectator sport. Rather, student and teacher were engaged in a process known as *mitori geiko*, "learning by watching." For this reason, they needed to pay close attention at all times and strive to add a layer of detail to their understanding and appreciation with each iteration. In his day, he added, instructors rarely made a point of teaching kata to the novices; rather, juniors would have to observe their seniors out of the corner of their eyes while performing some more menial exercise, so as to steal new techniques.

After a month or more, the new archers were permitted to fire their first arrows into makiwara. These straw bales were placed before them on wooden stands at a distance of no more than a bow length. Beginning at a range where it was impossible to miss ensured that the students' competitive instincts did not interfere with *kazu geiko*, (the process of internalizing the technique and coming to understand the cycle of movement). It was slow going, and the ambient humidity conspired with the students' dedication to destroy a number of makiwara, requiring frequent trips to the back of the long, narrow garage where the extra hay bales were stored. No one gave much thought to this minor inconvenience until the day of the fire.

The lesson was with the staff, not the bow that afternoon, and the class was arrayed on the lawn behind the dojo, sunlight reflecting brightly off their starched, white uniforms. It was a perfect autumn day for training: warm enough for comfort yet cool enough to ensure that active bodies did not overheat. The staffs sang through the air in unison. The master observed proudly. Then he stopped and cocked his head to

the side, that familiar, faraway look clouding his eyes. Those who knew him well could read his expression and glanced from side to side, straining to see what it was he had heard or sensed. Performance of the group form ground slowly to a halt, but the master did not seem to notice. He simply turned and began to walk briskly toward the dojo, like a blood-hound tracking its prey. A few moments later the students heard someone yell, "Fire!"

It seemed that the deliveryman who had brought the new bales of hay on his flatbed lorry had backed into the narrow garage for ease of unloading. He must have overshot his mark, for while he was in the administration building filling out the appropriate paperwork, the tailpipe of his vehicle had set the remains of the existing stock alight. Now both old and new loads were burning, along with the rear half of the delivery truck, and while the garage did not share a wall with the dojo, it was close enough to the lovely old building to place it in extreme danger.

Given the implied dismissal, the students ran toward the blaze as fast as their legs would carry them. One or two stumbled along the way in their haste. They arrived at the garage quickly, but once there, had no idea how to proceed. The master was nowhere in sight. A growing crowd of Japanese faces with a few Caucasians here and there looked on in horror as smoke poured from the garage door. For a few moments, nothing happened. It seemed no one knew what to do. Then the master arrived.

Walking, not running, he made his way steadily toward the scene. In his hands were some strips of blue cloth he had torn and wetted down along the way. He handed them out to a few of his students, gesturing that they should tie them over their noses and mouths as makeshift breathing masks. Calmly but firmly, he issued his orders. He told one of the secretaries to call the fire brigade and had the foresight to remind the young lady that the emergency number here was 999, not 110 or 911. He sent another to the campus gates to help the big engines negotiate the narrow passageway. He directed some of the students not to wet down the garage, but to wet down the thin strip of grass that separated it from the dojo, using a nearby hose. Then, tapping two of his most senior students on the shoulder, he strode into the smoke-filled cavern.

The delivery truck was blocking almost the entire width of the narrow structure. Rather than risk starting the engine, the master simply slipped the transmission into neutral and allowed the gentle slope of the floor to roll the vehicle out onto the lawn where it came to rest in the vicinity of the old cherry tree. His estimation of the effect of gravity in both starting and stopping the vehicle proved quite accurate, and a few bystanders managed to beat the flaming, wooden tailgate into submission.

Meanwhile, the three men in white uniforms worked

together to fight the fire within. The garage could not have been more than twenty feet long, but in the extreme heat and minimal visibility, it felt like a football field or more. One after another, they made the long trek down the smoke-filled passageway, dumping buckets of water onto the burning material and hauling out what they could. In the end they could not save the garage, but the adjacent building survived unscathed. In time, the charred skeleton of the structure was knocked down and the ashes ploughed into the soil where they made a fertile bed for the master's new garden.

Many years later, a reporter asked one of the three firefighters about the master. Who was he? The student started to answer, but as he did so, another image swam into his mind. He was driving home with his own son many years after the fire. He saw or sensed the neighbor's truck, with its failed hand brake, as it began to roll down the gentle slope toward the road. He doused the flames of rising panic and calmly but firmly explained to his boy that he would have to jump out and try to intercept the renegade truck before it gathered too much momentum. Their ultimate success in averting a disaster had been the presence of the master.

In that moment, the graduate understood the true answer to the question for the first time: "Who is the master?" he asked. "I am. You are. He is. She is. The master is in each of us. When a pilot brings a crippled aircraft safely to rest in an open field, it is the hand of the master on the yoke. When a teacher refuses to give up on a difficult student, it is the wisdom and patience of the master that provides the solution. And whenever a Good Samaritan answers the cry of an anguished soul, it is the voice of the master that speaks."

The reporter was perplexed; the student, enlightened.

55. *GYAKUTE* — THE UNEXPECTED

The wise man adapts himself to circumstances, as
water molds itself to the pitcher.

—Chinese proverb

Sparring with the master was very much like trying to dam
up a raging torrent with a single plank. Any defense one
mounted simply served as a median strip between two new
avenues of attack. It was impossible for his opponent to remain watertight for any length of time, and all the while, the
forward pressure mounted until his adversary was swept to
the wall or the floor in its inexorable tide. The secret, of
course, was his fluidity. Rather than consciously orchestrat-
ing an attack, a defense, or a counter, the master simply re-
acted to his partner's actions, flowing from move to move.
There was no need to evaluate, reconsider, or withdraw—his
technique was intuitive. It was Zen.

It takes an extraordinary level of competence to perform complex tasks instinctively. Most people have at least some passing familiarity with this phenomenon by virtue of certain mundane tasks that they carry out effortlessly on a daily basis. Driving a well-known route, tying one's shoes, or performing the simple act of placing one foot in front of another—these are all objectives that can be achieved without conscious attention. Put another way, few individuals can calculate the speed of a flying object, its rate of descent, and its relative distance with any great accuracy, but nevertheless, many can catch an infield fly on a good day. With sufficient study, more complex matters may be learned, digested, internalized, and performed instinctively. They may be mastered.

Like many of the principles the master taught, both by word and by example, this principle of flow has a wider realm of application. The odyssey of life frequently has its own destination in mind. Therefore, plotting an unwavering course is unwise as is insisting on driving forward regardless of the consequences. Rather, the wise man remains flexible, adaptable, and open to alternatives. The opportunity that arises is not always in the direction we expect. The real test may not be the one for which we have prepared. It is there nevertheless. Flow with it.

56. *HOKOSAKI* — ADVANCE AND BE RECOGNIZED!

The hunter can make many mistakes, the hunted, only one.

—Native American proverb

There is a time to yield and a time to mold. There is also a time to advance. Having exhausted less aggressive options, one will occasionally be faced with no alternative but to fight. By virtue of having followed the master's approach, such engagements will generally take the form of a defensive action, but there are situations when offensive measures may be required. Whatever the strategic nature of the opening stages of the battle, capturing the initiative in a tactical sense at an early stage, is vital.

Mao Zedong and Che Guevara understood that a small group of insurgents could easily occupy a much larger force if they kept it in a state of constant reaction. Furthermore, an enemy who is concerned with maintaining a defensive perimeter is easier to contain and eventually to defeat. Empires expand to a certain point and then collapse. It is the way of things. According to the master, there are several approaches to taking the initiative:

- From a pragmatic point of view, *sen-no-sen*, "the first initiative," can be a devastating tactic. A prime example of this principle in action occurred during the so-called Six-Day War in June 1967. Knowing that an attack was imminent, Israeli fighter pilots struck first, disabling over two thirds of their enemy's air forces before the latter had even left the ground. The result was a swift victory, as the name of the campaign suggests. Inherent in this approach are certain risks, but the nature of the threat and the practices of the enemy sometimes demand such a stab at the heart with the point of the sword from the outset.

- *Go-no-sen*, "retaking the initiative," is a safer tactic, at least from a legal standpoint—for it is far more difficult (although not altogether impossible) for an initial aggressor to maintain the argument of self-defense. This approach, however, carries with it concomitant costs. In this method, according to the master, the warrior must wait for the initial attack, countering only at the last moment. Properly applied, this teaching allows for a legal and ethical as well as tactical victory.

  An instructive example of the value of this approach, more the result of circumstance than planning, might be the Battle of Midway. In June 1942, Japanese carrier groups set out in force to attack the American outpost at Midway Island. Thanks in part to superior signals intelligence, U.S. air forces were able to intercept the fleet before it arrived and commenced a costly torpedo-bomber attack. Virtually all the aircraft in this first wave were lost, but for this price, they were able to recapture the initiative, and within minutes a second wave of American dive-bombers crippled three of the four Japanese carriers. Most historians agree that this one-day battle reversed the tide of war in the Pacific.

- The most difficult of these teachings is *tai-tai-no-sen*, "the simultaneous attack." The master of *aiki* can overwhelm an opponent with strength of spirit alone. This level of expertise is only rarely glimpsed at the highest levels of practice, but a powerful entry into simultaneous engagement, supported by a resolute spirit, can overwhelm even superior forces, thereby seizing the initiative. In June (a good month for spectacular victories it would seem) 1314, Edward II marched north with an army of 40,000 under his command, to crush the rebellious highlanders at Stirling. Scarcely 13,000 Scots, deployed in schiltroms[1] and under the command of Robert the Bruce, lay in wait at a narrow gap near the Bannock Burn. Wave after wave of English cavalry charged to their deaths, choking the pass with the fallen, but the defenders held fast. As the English began to falter, the Scots infantry made an unprecedented charge into the midst of the retreating cavalry. At the end of the day, English losses outnumbered Scottish twenty to one.

- In a broader sense, it is even possible to retain the initiative when the campaign must be conducted along

---

1. A circle of pikemen in formation, making an impenetrable wall of spears.

purely defensive lines. Consider, for example, the trial, imprisonment, and eventual execution of Sir Thomas More. When Henry VIII ordered all British nobles to sign the Act of Succession, declaring the king head of the Church in England, More quietly declined, rejecting this as a betrayal of his beliefs. He was locked away in the Tower of London for many seasons, and periodically debated, interrogated, and tortured some say, all in an effort to obtain his blessing. Throughout his ordeal, More stood by his convictions. So great was the character of the man and so respected his reputation that this struggle occupied some of the most powerful men of sixteenth-century England. In the end, the might and majesty of the British church and state was reduced to perjury in order to claim a Pyrrhic victory. This was so because one man refused to relinquish the high ground. He maintained the initiative.

57. *OKUNOTE*—THE OTHER HAND

I retrod the steps of knowledge along the paths of time and exchanged the discoveries of recent inquirers for the dreams of forgotten alchemists.

—Mary Shelly

To the master's way of thinking, one must not become bound up in so-called indoor technique. As a result, he would sometimes convene his senior classes on the forgiving sod of the university's Botanic Gardens, just off Hills Road. Even when it rained, there was an enormous tree whose wide canopy afforded the small group enough room to train while keeping them relatively dry. Occasional passersby would stop to watch the proceedings before moving on to the hothouse flowers display.

Out of courtesy to the other visitors, these classes were unobtrusive—there was no audible *ki-ai* or counting aloud of repetitions. But the overt tranquility of these sessions belied a deeper intensity, for it was particularly in this setting the master could be prevailed upon to share hitherto closely guarded teachings. It seemed that this too was a matter of *hyoshi*, "timing."

On one occasion, a violent thunderstorm swept across the pastoral background, and the skies darkened. Many of the students retreated out of habit into the arms of the old tree. The master, however, remained in the open, his sleeves popping in the rising wind and his eyes strangely bright. He beckoned to his senior student, inviting an attack. A moment later the young one sailed across the expanse of green, tucking into a defensive roll just before impact. The master called for another, and another, and another. His power seemed to grow in concert with the elements as a circle of opponents descended on him. The torrential downpour partially obscured visibility, but it was clear that he was now dispatching his attackers with the lightest of touches. At length, the master held up a single hand, punctuated by the first sharp crack of thunder. His assailants froze in place. The storm was far from over, but the lesson had ended.

As the saturated students made their way toward the wrought iron exit, the master murmured, "These things cannot be put in words." Despite his pronouncement regarding the futility of trying to capture the mysteries of his demonstration with mere pen and ink, lights burned brightly in dormitory rooms late into that night and the following morning.

58. *MATSUNEN*—THE FINAL DAYS

To finish a work? To finish a picture? What nonsense!
To finish it means to be through with it, to kill it, to rid
it of its soul, to give it its final blow, the coup de grâce
for the painter as well as for the picture.

—Pablo Picasso

The last few days with the master had an altogether different feel. A kind of distance between West and East seemed to
be reemerging. It was rumored that the admission of foreigners into this otherwise homogeneous tradition had not met
with favor in certain circles. Perhaps it was simply that the
master knew that time with his Englishmen was growing
short. In any event, the students certainly had no desire to
pry into his private thoughts. To do so would have been in
contravention of his teachings.

The final class was highly unusual. After the opening

formalities had been observed, the master banished the younger students to the *shimoseki* to work together on their assigned techniques. He himself withdrew to kamiza, with his writing table, leaving a handful of seniors at *joseki*. They were a mixed bunch—several highly skilled Japanese in their teens and a few *gaijin*, slightly older and certainly less polished. "Show me what you have learned," he commanded. For a moment, nothing happened. In a culture that prioritized order, the nonspecific nature of this command was something of an anomaly.

Through a form of visual telepathy typically developed among frequent testing partners, the upperclassmen fell into an erratic version of taiso, the warming-up routine, led by no one in particular. The master seemed indifferent. They progressed through repetitions of kihon and kata. The master remained aloof. Finally, they broke off into pairs and began *randori*. There was no visible reaction.

While fighting, the seniors were careful to keep a watchful eye out for any errant junior who might inadvertently stray into the line of fire. One particular combatant was repeatedly distracted from his matches by the sight of a younger student's determined efforts to slice open his hand with an improper "clamshell" drawing of his sword. This concern prompted him to glance to the master for some sign of appreciation of the imminent danger, but none was apparent. At the next opportunity, the student looked again to kamiza, quite surprised that this threat had somehow escaped the master's seeming omniscience. The master studiously avoided his gaze.

At last, unable to contain his concern any longer, the elder student bowed curtly to his opponent to excuse himself and scurried over to the shimoseki to whisper the necessary correction. The master looked up sharply. The students froze in place, each wincing internally at the perceived affront. For a moment the master's reaction was unclear. Then he nodded once, rose, and simply walked off the mat and out of the training hall.

Still no one moved. The seniors looked curiously to one another for guidance. None was quite sure what had just happened. However, one thing was clear: they were now on their own. After a time, the clock's second hand began to tick again, and the pairs began to dissolve, making their way to the far side of the dojo to take the class in hand. Over the

space of perhaps an hour, each shared with the expectant juniors some aspect of a technique or insight into a principle earned by long hours on the mat and paid for with blood and sweat.

Eventually, training was concluded and the closing ceremony observed. The class bowed to an empty kamiza. The students changed and filed silently out of the dojo, many for the last time. In the darkened room, the master's writing table sat undisturbed next to his swords. On it was a sheet of *hanshi* painted with a single symbol: kishi—an English knight.

59. *RENZOKU* — PASSING THE TORCH

Take up our quarrel with the foe.

—John McCrae

At the end of their tenure, the students departed from that special place and scattered on the winds. The master gave to each a parting gift. In a classic reversal of tradition, he chose

195

to offer them keppan at the conclusion of their studies rather than to demand it at the outset. He knew that an oath taken voluntarily and directed to oneself would be far more binding than any promise extracted by another. In exchange for sharing his tradition with outsiders, gratis, and at considerable risk to his own position, he asked only one thing—that each commit to the fundamental ideals he had striven to impart.

Which specific techniques and arts he had taught were of relatively little consequence—they were, after all, nothing more than a vehicle. What mattered was the manner in which they were applied. On a single sheet of thick white paper he had inscribed seven symbols—gi, yu, jin, rei, makoto, meiyo, chugi. An empty circle was at the bottom in which the student could make his mark, if he so chose, and thereby bind himself to this code. The master never asked. It was a matter of principle.

The old man observed the foreigners' peculiar commencement ceremony from a distance. As the don recited the list of graduates in his strange and nasal tongue, certain names were familiar. At their mention, the old one nodded slightly. He remained on the hillside until the last of them had reunited with family and friends, dissolving into the boisterous crowd. Then he made his way gently down the far slope toward his cottage and the tiny garden that lay beyond.

He intended to begin pruning back a new growth of particularly vigorous hibiscus. He rested his staff against the trunk of the old cherry tree. At the tip of one of the high branches, a single blossom finally detached itself and fluttered lazily to the ground at the master's feet. He smiled to himself for a moment—then turned his attention back to the unruly bushes. This would take some time.

60. *OKU NO HOSOMICHI* — THE NARROW ROAD TO A FAR PROVINCE

Years fell away from the calendar like leaves from a tree in the first caress of fall; slowly at first but rapidly gathering momentum. Student and master met again while still in their respective primes, in a darker and very different context, but that is another book. This is the story of the end.

Time had almost caught up with the old man. He was lying on a futon, propped up in place by a few small pillows. The frailness of his withered body betrayed the razor-sharp intellect that remained trapped within. In his final hours, he was surrounded by the family and loved ones who had known him best, but in another way not at all.

When the student arrived, he was greeted with an appropriate measure of respect and warmth by those who had summoned him on the master's behalf, and yet there still remained a certain distance. It was a sign not just of cultural differences, but also a sense of spiritual otherness. This was the foreigner of whom the master sometimes spoke; the one he had allowed into a part of his life about which few others had even known.

When his visitor arrived, the master asked that they be left alone. Friends and family dutifully filed out of the room to make a space appropriate to the dimensions of the encounter that was to follow. Despite his diminished state and limited time, the master had immediately focused on the needs of the student, guiding him one final time through the exercise of mastering his own mindscape.

This stark realization roused the student from his reverie. He looked to the master—his master—ashamed. Ashamed for a thousand failings over the years. For the sins of selfishness, sloth, stupidity, and skepticism. He opened his mouth to speak, but no words came. The master rested his hand heavily on the student's forearm. "I know," he said.

In that moment, the student finally and fully came to understand that their kindred spirits had been together from the very beginning, even before the first time they met. The old man's breathing was labored now, and his fractured English was further hindered by an ominous and persistent rattle emanating from the back of his throat. It was clear that he had only moments left. With the last of his breath, he completed the thought, closing the circle, and leaving the student—his favorite student— with the ultimate gift: ". . . And just as I was with you in the beginning, so I will be with you until the very end . . ."

He did not speak again. They sat in silence for a while. As the early morning twilight began to yield its domain to the dawn, a gnarled hand slipped from the student's sleeve and dropped onto the tatami as effortlessly and finally as a sheaf of snow sliding from the cradle of a broad leaf in the warmth of the rising sun. And in the cup by the master's bed, the gently swirling mixture silently resolved itself into the two elements from which it had originally been formed.

GLOSSARY

Note: This glossary is designed primarily to assist readers unfamiliar with certain Japanese martial arts terms in making their way through the text of this book. Definitions are deliberately brief and lack any exploration of the nuances critical to a comprehensive understanding of these words. Volumes have been written on any number of the terms provided below, and these abbreviated references may serve only to whet the appetite for further examination of the subject matter. Terms provided in this glossary are generally Japanese unless otherwise indicated.

Aiki: Variously translated as "Blending energies," or "energy!"

Aikido: A soft style of martial arts founded by Morihei Ueshiba.

Aikuchi: A small, hiltless dagger used in martial arts.

Anza: A manner of sitting with legs crossed in front.

Bajutsu: The samurai art of equestrianism.

Bokken: A wooden practice sword.

Bonsai: The Japanese art of cultivating miniature trees.

Bujutsu: Martial arts.

Bushido: The way of the samurai.

Chado: The way of tea, the tea ceremony.

Chugi: Loyalty.

Chushingura: The Forty-seven Faithfuls.

Daichi: A plateau, as with a mountain.

Daimyo: A feudal lord.

Daisho: A matching pair of Japanese swords (literally: large-small).

Daito Ryu: A style of aikijujutsu founded by Minamoto Yoshimutu.

Deshi: Student or disciple.

Docere: Latin: to teach.

Dojo: A training hall (literally: Way-place).

Doka: Poems of the Way.

Ducere: Latin: to lead.

Ei: A fundamental character encompassing the principle strokes in shodo.

Enkyoku: Euphemistic; circumlocution; roundabout; indirect; insinuating.

Enso: A circle.

Eta: Untouchables, outcasts, the lowest order of society.

Feng shui: The Chinese art of placement or geomancy (literally: wind and water).

Fudoshin: The quality of constancy or immovability.

Garyotensei: A Japanese idiom meaning to put on the finishing touches.

Genri: A principle, theory or fundamental truth.

Gestält: German: a term used in psychology to indicate a holistic approach.

Gi: Right decision.

Giho: A tactic, tactics.

Giri: Societal or conventional obligation.

Gogyo: The five elements employed in Eastern cosmology.

Gomuyumi: A practice bow used in kyudo.

Go-no-sen: The tactic of recapturing the initiative.

Hachimaki: A cloth or towel worn on the head beneath a kendo helmet.

Haiku: A form of epigrammatic Japanese poetry.

Hanare: The stage in kyudo at which the arrow is loosed.

Hanshi: Rice paper used in shodo.

Happogiri: Eight fundamental cuts in Japanese swordsmanship.

Hassetsu shaho: The eight positions of the archer.

Heiho: A stratagem, strategy.

Honza: An observation stage in kyujutsu.

Ich . . . ni . . . san: One . . . two . . . three.

Ichigo, ichie: "One encounter, one opportunity."

In/yo: Japanese for yin/yang.

Itto Ryu: A linear style of swordsmanship.

Ius cogens: Latin term meaning higher law (literally: compelling law).

Jin: Benevolence.

Jo: A medium-length staff.

Joseki: The senior half of a dojo (side to side).

Jutte: A truncheon sometimes used for trapping a sword's blade.

Kamiza: The senior side of a dojo (front-back).

Kanji: Japanese characters (originally derived from Chinese script).

Kata: A prearranged set of martial arts techniques, usually performed solo.

Katana: A Japanese sword.

Katate: One-handed grip.

Kendo: The sport of Japanese swordplay.

Kenjutsu: The art of Japanese swordsmanship.

Kenjutsu-ka: A practitioner of kenjutsu.

Keppan: A blood oath, sometimes required when joining a martial arts school.

Ki-ai: The focusing of energy in a technique, often accompanied by a yell.

Kihon: Basic or fundamental techniques.

Kishido: The Way of the Western Warrior (literally: The Way of the English knight).

Koan: Seemingly paradoxical or nonsensical stories, propositions, or questions intended to assist in the process of meditation and the search for enlightenment.

Kochou-jutsu: The art of influencing things and people indirectly.

Kohai: A subordinate or junior.

Koryu: Traditional or classical style.

Koshi mawari: Hip rotation.

Kotan: Elegant simplicity.

Kuden: An oral teaching.

Kumitachi: A two-person prearranged sword form.

Kuzushi: Breaking the balance of an opponent.

Kyudo-ka: A practitioner of kyudo.

Kyusho-jutsu: The martial art of striking pressure points.

Lingua franca: In Latin, a medium of communication between people of different languages.

Logres: Another term for the kingdom of Arthur. Sometimes used to describe the tenets or philosophical belief system upon which the Kingdom of Camelot was based.

Makiwara: A target for striking or short-range shooting.

Makoto: Truth.

Mato: A long-distance target used in kyudo.

Mayday: A corruption of the French term "m'aidez," used in aviation emergencies.

Meiyo: Honor.

Mitsu-tomoe: An Okinawan symbol composed of three comma shapes.

Mokuso: Meditation.

Ninjo: Personal desire, wish, or feeling.

Nyujo: A preparatory stage in kyujutsu.

Obi: A thick belt worn in martial arts training.

Oi tsuki: A stepping or lunging punch.

Oku: Interior or hidden aspect. When used as a noun, a secret teaching.

Omote: The outer or superficial aspect of a thing.

On: A notional obligation or debt.

Penjing: A Chinese form of bonsai.

Post hoc ergo procter hoc: Latin: after this, therefore because of this (a logic term).

Randori: Free sparring.

Realpolitik: German: a term used to describe a pragmatic view in political science.

Rei: Right action.

Reiki: A Japanese healing art involving touch therapy.

Reishiki: Ceremonial or formal behaviors or traditions.

Renga: A form of Japanese linked verse.

Ronin: A masterless samurai (literally: wave man).

Roshi: A koan master or teacher.

Ryu: A martial tradition or lineage.

Sadamenoza: A contemplative stage in kyujutsu.

Sai: An Okinawan weapon shaped like a trident.

Sake: A potent Japanese rice wine.

Saki: The tip of a weapon, usually a staff.

Sakibouchi: The cat's paw strike.

Samurai: A member of Japan's noble-warrior class.

Sang-froid: French: cold-blooded.

Satori: Enlightenment.

Saya: A sword's scabbard.

Seiza: A manner of sitting with the calves tucked under the thighs.

Sempai: A superior or senior.

Sen-no-sen: The tactic of taking the initiative from the outset.

Sensei: Teacher (literally: one who has lived before).

Sensu: A Japanese folding fan.

Seppuku: The process of self-immolation commonly referred to as hara-kiri.

Shaho: A Japanese archery range.

Shiai: Sparring.

Shihan: A term for master.

Shika: A generic term for Japanese and Chinese poetry.

Shimoseki: The junior half of a dojo (side to side).

Shinai: A bamboo practice sword.

Shin-jutsu: Acupuncture.

Shinza: A shrine or shelf for venerated or symbolic objects in a dojo.

Shodo: Japanese calligraphy.

Shoji: A paper screen.

Shotokan: A style of karate founded by Gichin Funakoshi.

Shugyo: Austere training methods.

Sine qua non: Latin: a term meaning essential (literally: without which not).

Stat: Latin: a term for "immediately," or "urgent," used in the medical field.

Suburito: A heavy wooden practice sword.

Taiso: Stretching or warming-up exercise.

Tai-tai-no-sen: The tactic of simultaneous attack.

Tameshigiri: Test cutting with a sword.

Tanren: Prolonged exercise.

Tanto: A Japanese dagger.

Tatami: A straw mat used in Japanese homes and martial arts training.

Te: An ancient term for the self-defense art of Okinawa.

Tokonoma: A shrine or alcove for displaying venerated or symbolic objects.

Tsuka: The grip or handle of a sword.

Uchine-jutsu: The largely forgotten art of using the unstrung bow as a staff.

Uneri: A winding or wave motion; the symbol of Kishido.

Voir dire: French: a term used at law in reference to jury selection.

Wakizashi: A Japanese companion or short sword.

Washi: Paper.

Waza: A technique, techniques.

Ya: An arrow.

Yabusame: The samurai art of shooting a bow from horseback.

Yajiri: An arrow tip.

Yin/yang: The two fundamental aspects of the universe, light-dark, positive-negative.

Yu: Bravery.

Yumi: A Japanese longbow.